ANDREW MURRAY

on the

HOLY SPIRIT

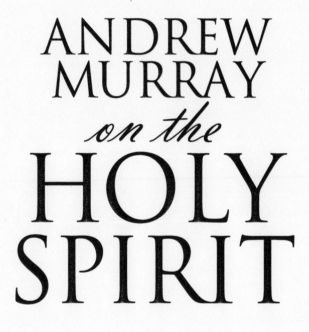

ANDREW MURRAY

on the

HOLY SPIRIT

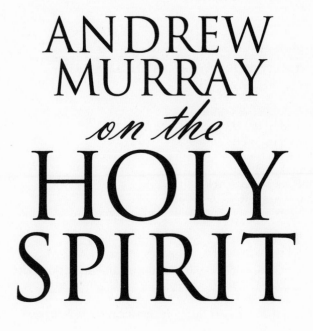

WHITAKER
HOUSE

All Scripture quotations are taken from the King James Version (KJV) of the Holy Bible.

Editor's note: This book has been edited for the modern reader. Words, expressions, and sentence structure have been updated for clarity and readability.

ANDREW MURRAY ON THE HOLY SPIRIT

ISBN: 0-88368-846-8
Printed in the United States of America
© 1998 by Whitaker House

Whitaker House
30 Hunt Valley Circle
New Kensington, PA 15068
visit our web site: www.whitakerhouse.com

Library of Congress Cataloging-in-Publication Data

Murray, Andrew, 1828–1917.
  Andrew Murray on the Holy Spirit / Andrew Murray.
    p.   cm.
  ISBN 0-88368-846-8
  1. Holy Spirit. I. Title: On the Holy Spirit. II. Title.
  BT121.3 .M87 2002
  231'.3—dc21
                                        2002012165

  1 2 3 4 5 6 7 8 9 10 11 12 / 09 08 07 06 05 04 03 02

Contents

1

The Kingdom
of God

1

The Kingdom of God

✦══✦══✦

*Verily I say unto you, Whosoever shall not
receive the kingdom of God as a little child,
he shall not enter therein.*
—Mark 10:15

When Christians gather for a convention in a new place, the first
meeting is often a difficult one.
Most of the people are strangers to each other.
An atmosphere of prayer and love has hardly
yet been created. There is uncertainty as to
whether everyone understands the purpose of
the meeting. But rest assured, the Father in
heaven can melt many hearts into one. By His
Holy Spirit, the Father can make them all of

one heart and one mind in seeking His glory, in trusting His mighty power, and in looking to Him alone for a blessing.

We must look to God at all times, not only for what each one needs for himself, but also as members of one body, with the fervent prayer that there may be a blessing for all. Let us unite ourselves before God as a company of His own dear children, full of love for each other and with the confident assurance that He will bless us.

A Prayer

Our Father, melt our hearts into one by Your Holy Spirit. You know the need of each one; let Your Word meet it. May Your children know what their God has for them and what they may expect Him to do for them.

Look closely at our text verse in Mark 10:15: *"Verily I say unto you, Whosoever shall not receive the kingdom of God as a little child, he shall not enter therein."* Read that verse again. As you begin reading this book, look forward to all that you are going to learn, and try to take your right place before God. I think this word of the Lord Jesus will guide you exactly to where you ought to be. It will tell you what

God asks of you if you are to enter His kingdom and live in it: you must receive it into your heart as a little child would.

There are two things you need to know to enter into the enjoyment of a full salvation: the wonderful blessing God has for you and the wonderful way in which you are to become a possessor of it. These two things will be the focus of this chapter.

My text verse has four simple expressions that we need to understand if we are to enter into its meaning and power. We must ask the following questions:

1. What is the kingdom of God?

2. What does it mean to enter the kingdom?

3. What does it mean to receive the kingdom?

4. What does it mean to receive it as a little child?

What the Kingdom Is

First, what is the kingdom of God? You know that John the Baptist preached that the kingdom of God, or the kingdom of heaven, had come. During the Old Testament times, it had been spoken of and promised and hoped for, but it had not come. During the life of Christ on earth, there were great signs of its coming and its nearness, but it had not yet come in power. Christ foretold what it would be when He said, *"The kingdom of God is within you"* (Luke 17:21), and another time, *"There be some standing here, which shall not taste of death, till they see the Son of man coming in his kingdom"* (Matt. 16:28).

On the Day of Pentecost, that word was fulfilled. The Holy Spirit brought the kingdom of God from heaven and into the hearts of the disciples. Then the disciples went forth and preached the Gospel of the kingdom, not as if it were coming, but as if it had come.

It is not difficult now to answer the question, What is the kingdom of God? It is that spiritual state in which the life of God and of heaven is made accessible to men, and they enter into its enjoyment here on earth. If we ask what the signs of it are, we find the answer in the wondrous change that took place in the lives of the disciples.

The King's Presence

The first sign of a kingdom is the presence of its king. With the Holy Spirit, Christ came down to be with His disciples as truly as when He was with them in the flesh. The Spirit was also nearer to the disciples than Christ could be in the flesh. The abiding nearness and fellowship of Christ, and of God the Father through Him, is the very central blessing of the kingdom.

This experience was what the Holy Spirit made real at Pentecost. The disciples had their Lord with them as consciously as the angels in heaven have Him. His presence put heaven all around them and in them. When a believer is given a full entrance into the kingdom, he has the presence of God and Christ as the *good part, which shall not be taken away* (Luke 10:42).

The King's Rule

Another sign of a kingdom is the rule of its king. We read, *"His kingdom ruleth over all"* (Ps. 103:19). Before Pentecost, the disciples could not love or be humble, could not trust or be bold. But when the kingdom came, the dominion of God prevailed, God's presence through the Holy Spirit gained the victory, sin was overcome, and the will of God was done in them as it is in heaven. When Jesus taught them to pray, *"Thy kingdom come. Thy will be done in earth, as it is in heaven"* (Matt. 6:10), He promised this.

As the kingdom came down with the Holy Spirit, the promise was fulfilled. And our entering into the kingdom means our being brought into a life in which God rules over all, His will is truly and joyfully done, and all the blessedness that reigns in heaven finds its counterpart here below. As it is written, *"For the kingdom of God is...righteousness, and peace, and joy in the Holy Ghost"* (Rom. 14:17).

Power

A third mark of a kingdom is power. *"The kingdom of God is not in word, but in power"* (1 Cor. 4:20). Just think of the work those simple fishermen dared to undertake and were able to accomplish. Think of the weapon with which they had to do their work—the despised Gospel of the crucified Nazarene. Think of all that God brought about through them, and see how the coming of the kingdom brought a new power from heaven. By this power, feeble men were made mighty through God, and the slaves of Satan were made God's holy children.

Believers, it is this kingdom of God come from heaven that I preach. I come to tell you that a life in the presence, the will, and the power of God has been opened up; that men have been given the opportunity to enter into it and live in it; and that you, too, can enter in.

Perhaps some of you are confessing the feebleness of your Christian lives and the failure of all your efforts to make it better. You have believed in Jesus as your Savior, but you know nothing about an entrance into the kingdom as it came in power. I urge you to begin today. Believe that here on earth you can live such a life in the kingdom. Believe that Christ's death brought about such a wonderful and complete redemption and that the coming down of the Holy Spirit—nothing less than the glorified Christ coming in the Spirit— brought down the heavenly life in such reality that we can be *endued with power from on high* (Luke 24:49), just as the first disciples were.

If you will hold fast and believe that there is a kingdom of heaven on earth, your desire will be stirred to become a partaker of its blessedness. As I show you how you may do this, your hope will begin to see that this life is also for you. And you will be prepared to accept all that Jesus has to teach us in His Word.

Entering the Kingdom

What does it mean to enter the kingdom of God? This is our second question. You know the meaning of the word *enter.* It is most commonly used in Scripture to denote the entrance of the children of Israel into the Land of Promise and the believer's entrance by faith into the rest that God provides.

Entrance. The word simply means "coming into full possession or enjoyment." When Christ spoke of entering the kingdom of God, this is just what He meant and just what we long for with regard to the kingdom. The word does not refer to heaven or to our entering heaven when we die. Rather, it speaks of the kingdom of heaven upon earth and our entering into it in power as the disciples did at Pentecost.

There are many Christians who are content with having only a heaven after death. The promise of living in a kingdom of heaven here on earth has no attraction for them nor wakens any response in them. They cannot understand what this means. But there are many individuals in whom the longing has been awakened for something better and who would gladly know what it means, what it entails, to enter the kingdom.

As I said, *entrance* means "coming into full possession." Just think of the blessings of the kingdom: God's manifested presence is with us without ceasing; God's blessed rule and dominion are established over us, so that His heavenly will is done in us and by us; God's mighty power descends upon us, so that through us Christ can do His work of saving souls. Even now, you can enter into a life in which these blessings are your daily experience. That life has been prepared for you and is promised to you; it is waiting for you. You can enter it even now by faith.

As an army conquers and enters a city, so do many souls struggle and fight and seek to take the kingdom by violence. And they fail, because we can only enter by faith. As Joshua brought Israel into the Land of Promise, as Jericho fell without a blow being struck, so too does our Lord Jesus wait to bring us into the good land. It was He who, from heaven, gave the disciples their abundant entrance into the kingdom; it is He who, still by His Holy Spirit, will lead each one of us in. Because of our faith in Him, He brings us in.

You may want to know what this faith is and how it works. Know what our Lord tells us about receiving the kingdom.

Receiving the Kingdom

Our third question is, What does it mean to receive the kingdom? What is the difference between the two expressions our Lord uses, "entering the kingdom" and "receiving the kingdom"? You can see that He made the latter, receiving, the condition of the former, entering. The one is active: I enter in and take possession. The other is passive: I receive.

These words give expression to the great truth that, before I can enter the kingdom, it must first enter into me. Before I can possess its privileges and powers, it must first possess me, with all my powers and being. I must, in subjection and surrender, in poverty and emptiness, receive the kingdom into my heart before I am fit to be entrusted with all the power and glory it offers me. What is dark and evil within me must first be cast out; what is of God must fill my being. Only what is born of God alone can inherit the kingdom and its heavenly life. There must be a heavenly nature before there can be a heavenly position.

The message here is very simple: receive the kingdom. It implies that there is One who gives and another who accepts. So many people have heard of the blessed life of the kingdom and the wonderful joy it gives, yet they have never thought that it must be received from the living God Himself. What we need is to be brought to such consciousness of our utter ignorance and helplessness that we feel we cannot grasp or comprehend this wonderful salvation that is offered. We are to come into contact with the Father in heaven and, as a heavenly gift, receive from Him the kingdom in power.

And this is not something that we have to persuade Him to give us. Instead, it is the child's portion that actually belongs to us and that He wants to see us enjoy. As we believe this, and as we look up to the everlasting God who is infinitely ready and able to give the kingdom in its power to our very hearts, our hearts will take courage and begin to expect that the kingdom with its blessings can indeed enter us.

Then our reception of it will become so simple. When we see the God who has promised, in His infinite love, to enter into us and to be everything in us, we will understand that our place is simply to rest in what He will do, to claim His great gift of the Spirit who brings the kingdom into us, and to wait in patient dependence for Him to do His mighty work. He desires to enter into our hearts, just as the sun with its light and life seeks to enter into every little flower and every blade of grass. Once we accept Him, our daily position will be that of counting on God to reveal and work in us all that He has for us.

You may be inclined to ask, "If the receiving is so simple, why is it still so difficult, and why do so few really find what they seek?" The answer is, The whole thing is so simple, but we are not simple. The simplicity of the thing is its difficulty, because we have lost our simplicity. This is what Jesus taught in the words that He spoke and what I must still speak of: *"Whosoever shall not receive the kingdom of God as a little child, he shall not enter therein."*

Becoming like Children

Finally, what does it mean to receive the kingdom of heaven as little children would? Do we have any illustration of this in nature? Yes. How do princes become heirs to the throne? They receive kingdoms by being born as little children. They are born to it. And so we must be born by the Holy Spirit into the disposition of heart, the childlike simplicity, that will receive the kingdom as a little child.

When a little child receives a kingdom, he does so as a feeble, helpless little thing. As he grows up and hears of what is coming to him, he does so in simple trustfulness and gladness. In a similar manner, Jesus calls us to become little children and, as such, to receive the kingdom.

Oh, how difficult it is for men and women, with their wills and their strength and their wisdom, with all the power of self and the *"old man"* (Rom. 6:6), to become like little children! It is impossible. And yet, without this we cannot enter the kingdom and its heavenly life. We can know about the kingdom, we may taste some of its powers, we may work for it and often rejoice in it, but we cannot enter in fully and entirely until we become like little children. *"With men this is impossible; but with God all things are possible"* (Matt. 19:26).

There are some things we can do to become like children. We can yield to the teaching of God's Spirit when He convicts us of our pride and self-reliance. We can confess our self-will and self-effort. We can pray and strive for the childlike spirit. We can go as far as Peter and the disciples did before Pentecost. But only the Holy Spirit, the Spirit of God's Son, the Spirit who cries, *"Abba, Father"* (Gal. 4:6), the Spirit who claims and expects and receives all from God alone, can give the little-child nature that enters into the kingdom. He is within you, as the Spirit of Christ, to bring this about. He gives the grace to become like a little child, and so He prepares the heart to receive from heaven His fullness, as He brings the kingdom in heavenly power.

How may you become like a little child? How can you lose all your strength and wisdom, your will and life, and be as a little, newborn child? "Oh, I wish I knew how!" you cry. Look to Jesus! As a babe in Bethlehem, He was born heir to the kingdom of David. He grew up to manhood, and then, giving up His will in Gethsemane when He cried, *"Abba, Father"* (Mark 14:36), He gave up His life and was laid in the dark grave in the helplessness of death. From there He arose as the *"firstborn from the dead"* (Col. 1:18), born again out of the dead to the throne of glory.

In the feebleness of the grave, Christ gained His throne. We need to die with Christ; that is the way to be delivered from the old man and self, the way to receive the heavenly life as a little child, and so to enter the kingdom. The feebleness of Bethlehem and the manger, of Calvary and the grave, was Christ's way to enter the kingdom. And the way for us is no different.

As we seek to humble ourselves and renounce all wishes and all hopes of being or doing good by our own powers, God's Spirit will cause the power of Christ's death and victory over sin to work in us. As we yield all our human abilities and energies in the confession that they are nothing but sinful and worthy of death, we will die with Him, and with Him we will be raised in *"newness of life"* (Rom. 6:4). This new life will be the little child that receives the kingdom.

The Life of Power

Oh, how little we see the kingdom of God come in power among God's children! Begin by asking yourself such questions as, How is it with me? Am I proving, in my own experience and to others, that the kingdom of God has come and that a child of God can enter in and live in all the blessedness of its heavenly life? Have I, through the Holy Spirit, received the kingdom into my heart so that the presence and power of God manifested in me and Himself working out His will in me and through me are indeed the strength and joy of my religion? Let nothing less than the possession of this satisfy you. Let this be your one desire.

To this end, let us hold fast to two things. The first is the unspeakable blessedness, the divine possibility, the absolute certainty of the kingdom of God in power being the privilege of God's people. Our hearts are meant to be the very dwelling places of God. The Holy Spirit is meant to be in us and through us so that all the action of the heart, all that is done by it, is done by the Holy Spirit inspiring it. The kingdom of heaven has come to earth and can be set up within us in such power that the presence, the will, and the power of God will be our life and joy. It is more than the mind can grasp: let us believe it. Our wonderworking God will make it true.

The other thing is this: let us believe that all that is needed to be in full possession of these blessings is what the Holy Spirit, who is already in us, will bring about. He will cause us to be like little children before God. He will enable us as such to receive the kingdom from the Father. He will lead us and bring us in so that we enter into the kingdom and the heavenly life it gives.

Can you not therefore say, "Lord, nothing less than this can satisfy me. I want to live my life fully in Your kingdom. I yield myself, I yield self with all its life, to You"? In the faith of the Holy Spirit, I say, "Here I am as a little child. Father, in the gift of Your Spirit in Pentecostal power, let me receive the kingdom as a little child."

2

The Indwelling
of God

2

The Indwelling of God

What agreement hath the temple of God
with idols? for ye are the temple of the
living God; as God hath said, I will dwell
in them, and walk in them; and I will be
their God, and they shall be my people.
—2 Corinthians 6:16

We have here an answer to the question, How is God going to be my
God? Am I to regard Him as a
great and almighty and distant God, outside
of me and separate from me in the heaven
above, from whom I am, from time to time,
to have a little help? That is what many

Christians think, and it is because of this idea of God that they experience so little of His real presence and power.

No, this thought of God is only the beginning of true faith in Him. As we learn to know Scripture better, and as we comprehend the deep need of our hearts and the wonderful love of God that is waiting to enter completely into us, we learn that there is something even better. The question, How is God going to be my God? finds its answer in the words of our text: *"God hath said, I will dwell in them,...and I will be their God."* That is God's answer to your question.

And what a wonderful answer it is! There are things that surround us and force themselves upon our notice and occupy our attention, but we never give them a place in our hearts. Then there are other things that enter into us and take possession of our lives. A mother has a place in her heart for her child. Similarly, the gold of a miser has his heart, with all its love and hope. We seldom think that our hearts were created so that God might actually dwell there, so that He might show forth His life and love there, and so that our love and joy might be in Him alone. How little we know that, just as naturally as we have the love of parents or children filling our hearts and making us happy, we can have the living God, for whom the heart was made, dwelling in our hearts and filling them with His own goodness and blessedness. This is my message: God wants your heart; if you give it to Him, He will dwell in it.

The psalmist referred to God as *"the God of my life"* (Ps. 42:8), *"the God of my strength"* (Ps. 43:2), *"God my exceeding joy"* (v. 4), and *"my God"* (Ps. 42:6, 11; 43:4–5). But how is God to be the strength of my life and my God? In no other way but by coming into my life with His divine life and so filling it with His almighty strength—then He is the strength of my life. With His holy life and love, He comes into my heart, into the very seat and center of my life, and acts within me as my God, working out my life for me. He makes divinely and bless-edly true what is written here: *"God hath said, I will dwell in them,…and I will be their God."*

Do you not think it would make a wonder-ful difference in our lives if we really believed this and, in believing, received the blessing it speaks of? What a holy awe there would be in us! And what a tender fear lest we should hurt or grieve this holy, loving God! What a long-ing would be awakened in us so that we would say, "I want to know how to walk with this God and have full communion with Him." And what a bright confidence would be ours so that we would exclaim, "Now my God has come to dwell in me; I do not need to fear any longer that I will not have His presence or that He will not do for me and in me all that I need!"

I want to write to you very simply about this wonderful indwelling. I want to give you a few thoughts that may help you to see that it is the very essence of true Christianity, the very thing man, as a sinner, needed to have restored to him, and the very thing Christ Jesus came to give.

Why Man Was Created

Let me say, in the first place, that man was created by God for nothing less, and nothing else, than this indwelling. Have you ever wondered why God created man at all? The reason was this: God brought creatures into existence so that He might show forth and impart His own divine goodness and glory to them in a way they could understand. And He desired that they, as far as they were capable of it, might share with Him His divine perfections and blessedness. He specially created man in His own image and likeness, so that in man He might show how the life of God could dwell in the human creature and gradually prepare him and lift him up for dwelling with God and in God through eternity.

God, in His love, said, "In his measure, I want man to be as holy and as good and as blessed as I am. I cannot give him the holiness or blessedness apart from Myself, but I can and will dwell in him, in the inmost depths of his life, and be to him his goodness and his strength." Yes, this was the glory of the divine creating love. God wanted to give man all He had Himself. God gave Himself to be man's life and joy.

In no other possible way could God do this but by dwelling in man. Just as an oil lamp has its light inside, and through the globe it gives off light all around, so the God of love created man so that He might be the light of his life. The dignity and blessedness of man was to be that all the glories of the blessed God would continually shine through him before the universe. Our natures, our wills, our inclinations, and our powers were all to be the vessels that would receive and hold and overflow with the blessed fullness of the life of God in us.

It was to be man's high prerogative and privilege just to offer and yield himself to God in the awareness of this holy partnership. Everything that God was in Himself in heaven, living out His own life there, He was to be the same on earth in and through man, living out His own life as truly as in heaven. Oh, the glory and the bliss of being man! Glory to God for our creation!

What Sin Has Done

But now, in the light of this blessed truth, *"I will dwell in them,"* look next at what sin has done. God made man to be His home, His temple, where His presence and His will would be all in all. But sin has robbed both God and us of this indwelling. The temptation with which Satan came to man in Paradise really meant this: would he with his whole heart yield to God as Father and Master, giving Him His place and doing His will alone? Or would he instead do his own will and let self rule as master in his own house? Oh, that fatal choice! God was dethroned and cast out of His temple, and self was set upon the throne.

Just as the image of an idol was set up in the very home that God Himself had caused to be built for us, so self was enthroned in the seat of God. The description of the man of sin, *"who opposeth and exalteth himself above all that is called God, or that is worshipped; so that he as God sitteth in the temple of God, showing himself that he is God"* (2 Thess. 2:4), is the true nature of self at every stage and in every state: self sits in the temple of God as God. All the sin of heathendom—how awful it is! All the sin of Christendom—no less terrible! These are simply the outgrowth of that one root: God dethroned, and self enthroned, in the heart of man. All the sin and sorrow of our lives has been nothing but this: we were not what we were created to be; we did not have God dwelling in our hearts to fill them with His life and peace and love.

Would you be content to have all kinds of snakes and insects occupying your house along with you? Or would you allow other people to be masters in the home in which you dwell? No, you never would. And yet, you allow so much else to occupy your heart and take the place God alone is meant to have. So many people are quite unaware that they are doing this. I write to you with this message: let there be an end of all this desecration of God's temple. God desires to have your whole heart for Himself. Oh, let it be given to Him.

The Work of Redemption

Third, in the light of this indwelling of God, let us look at Christ's work of redemption. What was the purpose of Christ's coming from heaven? It was to show us the possibility and the blessedness of being a man in whom God is living His life. We teach children by means of pictures and models. When God's Son became man, He lived a perfect human life as an illustration of the divine life in man: *"In all things it behoved him to be made like unto his brethren"* (Heb. 2:17). And Christ told us that He did this by the power of the Father dwelling in Him: *"I do nothing of myself; but as my Father hath taught me, I speak these things"* (John 8:28).

In Jesus, there was no question of abstract thought or deep theology. Here was a true man, sleeping, hungering, growing weary, being tempted, weeping, suffering as we do, telling us that the Father dwells in Him and that this is the secret of His perfect, blessed life. He felt it all just as we feel it, but He could do and bear all because the Father was in Him. He showed us how a man can live and how He would enable us to live.

When He had done this, He died so that He might deliver us from the power of sin and open up the way for us to return to God. On the cross He proved that a man in whom God dwells will be ready to suffer anything, and even give up his life, so that he may enter into the fullness of the life of God.

When sin entered into the world, man lost the life of God dwelling in him, and he became dead to it. There was no way for man to be freed from the life of sin except by dying to it. Christ died to sin so that He might take us up into His fellowship and so that we, too, might be dead to sin and might live unto God with His life. And so He won back for us the life that man had been created for—with God dwelling in him—by giving to us His life, the very life He had lived. He prayed, *"As thou, Father, art in me, and I in thee, that they also may be one in us"* (John 17:21).

Oh, my fellow Christians, this is the salvation that Christ has won for us: a deliverance from self by a death to it through the death on the cross, and a restoration to the life we were created for, with our hearts being a home for God.

Partaking of the Divine Life

Now, how are we to become partakers of this salvation? In the light of this blessed truth of the divine indwelling, look once again at Pentecost and the coming of the Holy Spirit. Have you realized what it means that God sent the Holy Spirit into our hearts? It is nothing less than this: Christ, who had been with the disciples on earth but not in them, came back to them in the Spirit, now to dwell in them just as He had before dwelt with them. All that we read of the wondrous change that came over the disciples—their selfishness changed into love, their pride into humility, their fear of suffering into boldness and joy, their unbelief into fullness of faith, their feebleness into power—was owing to this one thing: the glorified Christ had come to dwell within them as their Life.

That was the joy of Pentecost in heaven: God regained possession of His temples and could now again dwell in men as He had meant to do before the Fall. The temple that Christ said would be destroyed was the temple of His body, in its connection with our sin laid upon Him. The temple He was to build in three days was His resurrection body, with its holy, heavenly life. In union with it, we are now temples of the living God. The Holy Spirit takes possession in the name of the triune God, and the Father and the Son come to make their abode with us (John 14:23).

When we look at the great promise, *"I will dwell in them,"* and its fulfillment at Pentecost, we are reminded of the great difference between the preparatory working of the Spirit in conversion and regeneration and His Pentecostal indwelling. Every Christian must have the former, for without that there is no life. The life may be feeble and sickly, yet where there is life, it is the Spirit's working. But that is only to prepare the temple. Pentecost is the glory of God filling the temple, God coming to abide. Let us believe that the promise can and will be fulfilled.

Claiming the Promise

One more thought: in light of our text, look at the state of the church of Christ. There are so many believers of whom one would never say that their hearts are a temple that God has cleansed and where He dwells. There is a great deal of coldness and worldliness, self-ishness, sin, and inconsistency of profession of faith that makes one sometimes doubt whether there are Christians at all. The state of Christ's church is sad indeed. How little zeal there is for God's honor, how little delight in His fellowship or devotion to His service and kingdom, how little of a life in the power of the Holy Spirit! This surely proves that the promise, *"I will dwell in them,"* has never been understood or believed or claimed by a large majority of Christians.

Let me ask you, Have you claimed it? Do you seek to live it out? If not, my one objective here is to set before you this blessed life for which God has redeemed you, to urge and to help you to enter into it and walk in it.

Do I need to tell you how to do this? Begin by confessing how little you have even sought to live as God's temple. Think of how it must have grieved the love of your Father, that after all He has done through His Son and Spirit to regain His abode in you, you have cared so little to know about it or to seek it. Confess, too, your helplessness. You have tried to be better than you are, and you have failed. And you will fail until you receive His word that nothing less is needed, nothing less is offered, than for God Himself to become the strength of your life.

Set your heart upon the blessing. You know that desire is the great power that drives the world. Fix your desire upon this divine, wondrous grace, *"I will dwell in them."* Do not allow any thought of your unworthiness or feebleness to discourage you. This is something that is impossible with man but possible with God. He can and will fulfill His promise. Let it become the one desire of your heart. Understand that this is the salvation the Holy Spirit brings you as soon as you are ready to give up everything for it. As soon as the heart is ready to lose all, to be emptied of all, to be cleansed of all that is of self or nature, the promise will surely be fulfilled: *"I will dwell in them,...and I will be their God."*

Look now at the words that immediately follow my text: *"Wherefore come out from among them, and be ye separate, saith the Lord, and touch not the unclean thing; and I will receive you"* (2 Cor. 6:17). Come out from all that is of the world and from a worldly religion, from all that is inconsistent with the holy privilege of being God's holy temple and dwelling. Come out, and be separate. Take your stand as one who is going to live a life that is different from the crowd around you. Be separate unto God and His will. *"Touch not the unclean thing"* (v. 17). Be like a cleansed temple, where nothing that defiles in the very least may enter. Live wholly for God and holy to God, and He will make His word good: *"I will dwell in* [you]." He Himself will reveal and impart and maintain within you all that the promise means.

Believer, will you accept this full salvation? Will you do it now? I urge you, do not reject this wonderful love. Let your God have you, to satisfy His love and yours by dwelling in you. Accept it this moment, and you can trust Him to bring it about in you. Amen.

3

Jesus Christ in You

3

Jesus Christ in You

Examine yourselves, whether ye be in the faith; prove your own selves. Know ye not your own selves, how that Jesus Christ is in you, except ye be reprobates?
—2 Corinthians 13:5

I want to continue with the subject of the previous chapter: the indwelling of God. It is a topic of deep importance—one to which believers are in many cases so unaccustomed, and one that, even when its truth is accepted, cannot be understood in its fullness all at once. So it may be well to come back to it again.

Look again at the text verse for this chapter: *"Examine yourselves, whether ye be in the faith; prove your own selves. Know ye not your own selves, how that Jesus Christ is in you, except ye be reprobates?"* Every thoughtful Bible reader knows that the state of the Corinthian church was a very sad one. There were terrible sins among them, and both epistles to the Corinthians are full of sorrow and reproof.

At the close of the second epistle, Paul summed up all his pleadings in this one question: *"Know ye not?"* He may have been saying aloud as he wrote, "I fear you do not or else you would live differently. Do you not know that if you are not entirely condemned, Jesus Christ is in you?"

Like the text verse of the previous chapter, the words here teach us that the great truth that will lift a Christian out of sin and sloth is the promise of God's indwelling, the consciousness that Jesus Christ is in us.

"Know ye not your own selves?" Every Christian needs to know himself, not only his own sinfulness and helplessness, but especially the divine miracle that has taken place within him and made him the temple and dwelling of the triune God.

Above everything, do learn to *"know...your own selves,...that Jesus Christ is in you."* In every Christian community, there are numbers of people who are living low and feeble lives, without joy, without power over sin, or without influence to bless others. To all of these people, the message of Paul comes. Stop and think, and take in the wondrous thought that will be both the motivation and the power for an entirely new life: *"Christ is in you."* If you merely learn to believe this, to give way to it, and to yield yourself to Him, He will do His mighty saving work in you.

Assurance of Christ's Presence

This brings me to the two great questions that occupy Christians. The first is, Why do so many Christians fail? To this the answer comes: they do not know for sure that Jesus Christ is in them. Not one of us could live a worldly life, could give way to pride and self-ishness and temper, could so grieve the Holy Spirit of God, if he indeed knew that Jesus Christ was in him.

The effect of this knowledge would be simply wonderful. On the one hand, it would solemnize and humble a man and draw him to say, "I cannot bear the thought of grieving the Christ within me." On the other hand, it would encourage and strengthen him to say, "Praise God, I have Jesus Christ within me; He will live my life for me." May God bring us to the confession of how much we have lost because we lacked this faith. And may He teach us to pray often that, from moment to moment, our lives may have the assurance that Jesus Christ is in us.

How to Know Christ Within

Then comes the other question: If I find that I have not known and lived this life, am I ready to say today, "From now on, by the grace of God, I will live it. I can rest content with nothing less than the full experience of knowing that Jesus Christ is in me"? Let us come in deep poverty and emptiness. He who did the work for us so perfectly on Calvary undertakes to do it in our hearts, too. May God, by the Holy Spirit, reveal to each of us all that He means us to enjoy.

I have recently observed the lives of many young people. I want to write simply now, in order to help even the very youngest Christian to have some correct understanding of this blessed life that God has prepared for us. I want to address some of the questions that you may have concerning the indwelling of God, especially for those to whom it appears something too high and strange. Give your attention to these things, in the faith that God Himself will teach you.

Accept the Indwelling Christ

Let me say, in the first place, if you desire to know the power of this life, then believe in and accept the indwelling Christ. Let me ask you, Do you fully and truly believe in the indwelling Christ? You most likely believe in an incarnate Christ. When the name of Christ is mentioned, you at once think of One who was born as a little babe at Bethlehem, who took our nature upon Him and lived as a man upon earth. That thought is inseparable from your faith in Him.

You believe, too, in the crucified Christ, dying on Calvary for your sins. You also believe in the risen Savior, One who lives forevermore. And you believe in the glorified Lord, now sitting on the throne of heaven. But do you believe as definitely—as naturally—in the indwelling Christ? Have you made that one of the elements of your faith, as truly as you believe in Christ incarnate or Christ crucified? It is only as this truth is accepted and held fast that the others can really benefit you.

The experience of the love and the saving power of our incarnate, crucified, glorified Lord depends entirely upon His dwelling in us to reveal His presence and to do His work. If you find your spiritual life to be feeble or sickly, you may be assured that it is because you do not know that Jesus Christ is in you. Come to the Lord right now and begin at once to say, "I want with my whole heart to possess this wonderful knowledge, not as a doctrine, but as an experience. I want to know that Jesus Christ is in me." Begin to believe it at once. Accept Him, even now, as an indwelling Savior. Day by day, be content with nothing less than the blessed consciousness of His indwelling presence. He loves to reveal Himself.

To some extent, people always make their homes the expression of their tastes and characters. Similarly, for the heart that accepts and trusts Him to dwell within, the Lord Jesus brings it into sympathy and harmony with Himself. If you ask what the influence is that He will exert, the answer is not difficult: He becomes your life, and He will live in you. All that is implied in that wonderful word

life, all your thoughts and feelings and disposi-
tions and actions, will have His life and spirit
breathing in them. Oh, you Christians who
have never yet known in yourselves *"that Jesus
Christ is in you,"* believe in Him; accept Him
even now as the indwelling Christ.

Accept the Whole Christ

Here is a second thought: when you accept
Christ to dwell in you, be sure you accept the
whole Christ. There are some people who long
for the indwelling Christ but think of Him
chiefly as One who comes to comfort and
make glad, to bring peace and joy. But these
people do not accept Him in all His attributes
and offices. Beware of being content with only
half a Christ; see to it that you have the whole
Christ.

There are people who accept Christ as a
priest to atone for their sins but who do not
yield to His rule as a king. They never even
think of giving up their own wills wholly
and entirely to Him. They come to Christ for
happiness but not for holiness. They trust in
the work He has done for them, but they
do not surrender themselves to Him for the
work He is to do in them. They speak of the
forgiveness of sins, but they know little of

the cleansing from all unrighteousness. (See 1 John 1:9.) They have not accepted a whole Christ, who is the Savior from the power of sin as much as from the guilt of sin.

Let me urge you to make a study of this. As you read about the life of Christ on earth, take every trait of that holy character to be the will of God concerning you. Study His holy humility and meekness and say, "This is the Christ who dwells in me." Look at His deep dependence upon the Father; look at the perfect surrender of His will to do only what pleased the Father and say, "I have yielded myself so that my indwelling Lord may work this in me, too."

As you gaze upon Him as the Crucified One, not only think of the Cross in its atonement, as the means of propitiation for your sin, but also think of its fellowship as the means of victory over sin. Beware of only saying, "Christ was crucified for me"; say, too, "I am crucified with Christ." (See Galatians 2:20.) The one thing for which He lives in you is to breathe His own likeness into your nature, to impart to you His own crucifixion spirit, to give you the blessed disposition that made His sacrifice so well pleasing to the Father. Do accept the whole Christ as dwelling in you.

Especially, do not forget that the Christ who is in you is the Loving One, the Servant and the Savior of the lost. This is the chief evidence and glory of the Son of God, that He lived and died, not for Himself, but for others. When He comes to dwell in you, He cannot change His nature; it is the crucified, redeeming love of God that has taken possession of you.

Yield yourself to Him so that He may breathe into you His own love for souls, His own willingness to give up all so that they may be saved, and His own faith in God's almighty conquering grace. Do accept a whole Christ, a Savior from all sin and selfishness, a Savior, not only for yourself, but also for everyone around you.

Accept Him Wholeheartedly

My third thought is this: if you accept the whole Christ, accept Him with your whole heart. Nothing less than this can satisfy God, can secure Christ's full indwelling, or can give your heart rest.

This was what even the Old Testament demanded: *"Thou shalt love the LORD thy God with all thine heart,...and with all thy might"* (Deut. 6:5). To this action alone the promise was given: *"Blessed are they that...seek him with the whole heart"* (Ps. 119:2). The psalmist confessed, *"With my whole heart have I sought thee"* (v. 10). How can we think that this wondrous New Testament blessing—Jesus Christ, the whole Christ, in us—can be known in power, unless the whole heart is given to Him?

With Intense Affection. With the whole heart—what does that mean? First of all, the heart means love and affection. Our relationship to Christ must not only be that of devotion to His service and trust in His help, but also one of intense personal attachment. His heart toward us is all love; His work was and is nothing but the revelation of infinite love and tenderness; and nothing but love on our part can be the proof that we have really accepted and known His love.

After Peter had denied Christ, his restoration to Christ's favor and to his place as the shepherd of Christ's flock hinged on his answer to the thrice-repeated question, *"Lovest thou me?"* (John 21:15). We should never think that only women and children, or only monks and saints, may speak the language of tender, fervent love to the Savior. If we accept Him with the whole heart, let us cultivate an intense, personal love. Let us not hesitate to say often, *"Thou knowest that I love thee"* (John 21:15). The heart means love, and the whole heart means love with all our strength.

With the Will. The heart also means the will. Accept Christ with the whole heart; that is, give up your will entirely and absolutely to Him. Say to yourself that it is a settled thing, that you are never to seek your own will in anything. In things great and small, in decisions of supreme importance and in the most apparently insignificant questions of daily life, live as one who only exists so that the will of God and of Christ may be carried out in him. It was to do God's will that Christ came from heaven. It is to do God's will in you that He has entered your heart. Beware of hindering or grieving Him in this blessed work of His.

People sometimes ask, "Did God not give us a will so that we would use it? Is not man's nobility in the fact that he has a will? How can you ask us to give up that will so entirely and absolutely to God?" What a misunderstanding these questions imply! God gave us a will so that with it we might intelligently will what He wills. It is no degradation to a child to give up his will to be guided by a wise and loving father. So it is man's highest dignity to discover and accept and delight in the perfect will of God. Accept Christ with the whole heart and a perfect will; consider it your true and only blessedness to let Him breathe and work all God's will in you.

The whole heart means the whole will given up. Let this be the decision with which you bow to let His will rule: "Never my own will in anything." And let every sense of difficulty and feebleness only urge you afresh to believe that there is only one way of having your desire fulfilled, and that is by accepting Jesus Christ within you as an indwelling Savior. Accept Him as the living, inspiring power that breathes through all your will. You can have just as much of Christ as you give of yourself to Him; the whole heart can have the whole Christ.

When I have met with other pastors and preachers, the question often arises as to how to make our meetings more of a blessing to the people. One individual said that there seldom can be much blessing until there is first a great breaking down of self-sufficiency and pride, which leads Christians to feel how much is lacking in their lives. When I was in England last year, I heard about some meetings at which Christians were so convicted of the evil and shame of their Christian lives that, as they left the meetings, they hardly dared to speak, and they felt driven to go to God and confess their sins. This is what we need, what we cannot give ourselves, what only God can work in us.

Just as it is a matter of shame and humiliation when a wife has been unfaithful to her husband to whom she had pledged her whole heart, so is the thought that we have been guilty of withholding from God that undivided love to which He has such perfect right. Once we begin to see how we have been unfaithful to the all-glorious One, our Creator and our Redeemer, it ought to bow us down in the very dust. Then the sense of not having given the whole heart to Christ will become unbearable.

As we confess that we have not given God His glory, that we have sought our own wills and honor and pleasure, that we have given self and the world a place in the heart where Christ wanted to dwell alone, God's Holy Spirit can show us the sinfulness of our Christian lives. Then we will have no rest until we have said with full purpose and the assurance of divine approval, "I accept the whole Christ with my whole heart."

Count upon Him to Do All

Now comes the fourth thought. Count upon the indwelling Christ to do everything in your heart that needs to be done. In a verse just preceding our text, Paul said, *"Ye seek a proof of Christ speaking in me"* (2 Cor. 13:3). It was not only Christ living in him, but also Christ acting and speaking through him, that the Corinthian church looked for. The Corinthians were justified in that expectation. And so, when Christ comes in to take possession, He will by His Spirit do within us what we cannot do. He will make us what God wants us to be: conformed to the image of His Son.

It is utterly vain for us to think of following Christ's steps or imitating His example or copying His life by any effort of our own. Jesus lived a human life upon earth so that He might show us what the life is that we are to live. But it is foolish for us to think, now that we are Christians, that we can or will approach anything like His life on our own. It is impossible. We are indeed called to it. It is our first duty. But it can only come about if we let Him live that life in us. The life of Christ is altogether too high and too divine for us to reproduce. It is His own life, and only His, and He will live it out in us.

You want to be humble, patient, or gentle. You have often prayed and struggled, but it has all been in vain. You have sought humility here on earth, in yourself—something like what He, as God, brought from heaven. What foolishness! Oh, you must learn to cease from self and its efforts. Turn inward; let faith be occupied with and rest in the almighty, indwelling One, who has become the Possessor of your life for the very purpose of filling it with His own. Count upon Him who dwells within to do the work He has undertaken.

When He was on earth, Christ began His life as a little babe, unknown and very feeble. He grew up in seclusion, and no one thought that this was the Redeemer of men. When Jesus began His public ministry, He did not lift up His voice in the streets (Matt. 12:19); He was *"despised and rejected of men"* (Isa. 53:3); they did not know that He was *"the Lord of glory"* (1 Cor. 2:8). Similarly, within your heart, His appearance will be low and feeble and will hardly be seen.

Then the time will come to heed His command, *"Only believe"* (Mark 5:36). Trust in Him with an unmeasured confidence, that He will do His work within you in His own way and time. However slow and hidden and unlikely things seem to be within, hold fast to your confidence that He is there, that He is working, and that in due time He will reveal Himself.

Dear Christian, when you believe in the incarnate or crucified Christ, it means that you believe He perfectly did the work for which He came to live and die upon earth. When you believe in the risen and glorified Lord, it means that you have no shadow of doubt that He is now living and reigning at God's right hand, in divine power. Let your faith in the indwelling Christ be as simple and clear.

The work for which Christ entered your heart—the great work of possessing and renewing and glorifying your whole inner life—He will do in wondrous power and love. Trust Him for it. The Christ of Bethlehem, the Christ of Calvary, the Christ of the throne in heaven, is the Christ in you. Do begin to believe, "Jesus Christ is in me; He will do the work perfectly in me."

Think about that wonderful promise in the book of Hebrews:

> *The God of peace...make you perfect in every good work to do his will, working in*

you that which is wellpleasing in his sight, through Jesus Christ. (Heb. 13:20–21)

Yes, *"through Jesus Christ"!* If it is through Jesus Christ that God Himself works in you, how can this happen in any other way but by Jesus Christ Himself being in you? God enables you to do His will through Jesus Christ dwelling in you. Doubt no longer, but rejoice. *"Know your own selves...that Jesus Christ is in you."*

I am sure that some of my readers will ask, "Can this really be? Oh, if only I knew what is needed to have Christ Himself dwelling in me!" You will find the answer in the simple words, *"My son, give me thine heart"* (Prov. 23:26). Have you done that? Are you believers? Are you sure that your sins are pardoned? Are you seeking to live a Christian life?

Most of all, have you given your hearts to Christ so that He may possess them, rule them, renew them, dwell in them without rival, and fill them with the will of God? Have you given them away, out of your power and into His? Your self-confidence, your self-contentment, your self-pleasing, your self-will—have they all been laid at Christ's feet so that He can cast them out and fill your hearts with Himself? If not, let nothing keep you back from giving now what belongs to God and what Christ came to win back for Him. Your hearts were made for God.

A person has the wonderful power, in one moment, of setting his heart upon some object that strongly attracts him and of giving away his heart to it. At this moment, bow in penitence and shame that you have so little known that Jesus Christ is in you and that you have so little, day by day, yielded up your whole being to Him. Bow in lowly confession, offer Him even now your sin-stained and unworthy heart, and believe that He takes possession of it. What I give, God takes; what God takes, He will hold and keep through Jesus Christ. (See 2 Timothy 1:12.)

Blessed Lord, even now we give ourselves and know that You accept us, that You are within us, and that You will fill us with Yourself!

4

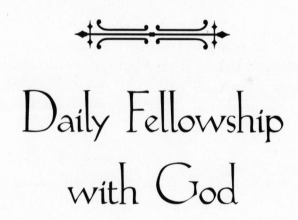

Daily Fellowship
with God

4

Daily Fellowship with God

✦━━•━━✦

So far I have been dealing with the divine life that comes to us when Christ dwells within our hearts. This divine life comes from God and is entirely dependent upon Him. Undoubtedly, the fellowship with God that accompanies this indwelling is the first and chief need of the Christian life. Just as I need fresh air to breathe every moment, just as the sun sends down new light every moment, so my soul can be strong only in direct, living communication with God.

The manna of one day was corrupt when the next day came. (See Exodus 16:13–20.)

Likewise, I must have fresh grace from heaven every day, and I obtain it only in direct waiting upon God Himself. Begin each day by waiting before God and letting Him touch you. Take time to meet God.

Be Still

To this end, let the first act in your devotions be to set yourself still before God. In prayer or worship, everything depends upon God taking the chief place. I must bow quietly before Him in humble faith and adoration. God is. God is near. God is love, longing to communicate Himself to me. The almighty God, *"which worketh all in all"* (1 Cor. 12:6), is even now waiting to work in me and to make Himself known. Take time, until you know God is very near.

Seek Humility

When you have given God His place of honor, glory, and power, take your place of deepest lowliness, and seek to be filled with the spirit of humility. As a creature, it is your blessedness to be nothing, so that God may be everything in you. As a sinner, you are not worthy to look up to God; you must bow in self-abasement. As a believer, let God's love overwhelm you and make you bow down still lower. Sink down before Him in humility, meekness, and patience, and surrender to His goodness and mercy. He will exalt you. Oh, take time to get very low before God.

Have Boldness and Assurance

Then accept and value your place in Christ Jesus. God delights in nothing but His beloved Son and can be satisfied with nothing less in those who draw near to Him. Enter deep into God's holy presence in the boldness that the blood gives and in the assurance that in Christ you are pleasing to Him. In Christ you are *"within the veil"* (Heb. 6:19). You have access into the very heart and love of the Father. This is the great objective of fellowship with God: that we may have more of God in our lives and that God may see Christ formed in us. Be silent before God, and let Him bless you.

This Christ is a living person. He loves you with a personal love, and He looks every day for the personal response of your love. Look into His face with trust until His love really shines into your heart. Make His heart glad by telling Him that you do love Him. He offers Himself to you as a personal Savior and Keeper from the power of sin. Do not ask, "Can I be kept from sinning if I keep close to Him?" but ask, "Can I be kept from sinning if He always keeps close to me?" and you will see at once how safe it is to trust Him.

Become More like Christ

We not only have Christ's life in us as a power and His presence with us as a person, but we also have His likeness to be worked out in us. He is to be formed in us, so that His form, His figure, and His image can be seen in us. Bow before God until you get some sense of the greatness and blessedness of the work that is to be carried on by God in you this day. Say to God, "Father, here am I for You to put into me as much of Christ's likeness as I can receive." And wait to hear Him say, "My child, I give you as much of Christ as your heart is open to receive."

The God who revealed Jesus in the flesh and perfected Him will reveal Him in you and will perfect you in Him. The Father loves the Son and delights to work out His image and likeness in you. Count upon it that this blessed work will be done in you as you wait on God and fellowship with Him.

The likeness to Christ consists chiefly of two things: *"the likeness of his death"* and *"the likeness of his resurrection"* (Rom. 6:5). The death of Christ was the consummation of His humility and obedience, the entire giving up of His life to God. In Him we are dead to sin. As we sink down in humility and dependence and entire surrender to God, the power of His death works in us, and we are made conformable to His death. And so, we know Him in the power of His resurrection, in the victory over sin, and in all the joy and power of the risen life. Therefore, every morning, *"yield yourselves unto God, as those that are alive from the dead"* (v. 13). He will maintain the life He gave and will bestow the grace for us to live as risen ones.

Seek the Spirit

All this can only be done in the power of the Holy Spirit who dwells in you. Count on Him to glorify Christ in you. Count on Christ to increase in you the inflowing of His Spirit. As you wait before God and begin to realize His presence, remember that the Spirit is in you to reveal the things of God. (See 1

Corinthians 2:10.) Seek in God's presence to have the anointing of the Spirit of Christ so truly that your whole life may be spiritual at every moment.

Surrender to God

As you meditate on this wondrous salvation, as you seek full fellowship with the great and holy God, and as you wait on Him to reveal Christ in you, you will feel how necessary it is to give up everything in order to receive Him. Seek grace to know what it means to live as wholly for God as Jesus did. Only the Holy Spirit Himself can teach you what an entire yielding of the whole life to God can mean. Wait on God to show you what you do not know in this matter. Let every approach to God, and every request for fellowship with Him, be accompanied by a new, very definite, and entire surrender to Him to work in you.

This must be done by faith. As through all Scripture and the entire spiritual life, this must be the keynote. As you wait before God, let it be in a deep, quiet faith in Him, the Invisible One, who is so near, so holy, so mighty, so loving. Let it also be in a deep, restful faith that all the blessings and powers of the heavenly life are around you and in you. Just yield yourself in the faith of a perfect trust to the ever blessed Holy Trinity, to work out God's entire purpose in you. Begin each day in such fellowship with God, and God will be all in all to you.

5

God Is Love

5

God Is Love

———✦———

God is love; and he that dwelleth in love
dwelleth in God, and God in him.
—1 John 4:16

How little we know what we are! It amazes me to think that the ever-lasting God, who created heaven and earth, deals with each one of us individually—He deals with *me*. And I am filled with wonder that it pleases Him to take from the fountain of His everlasting Godhead and fill me with His everlasting love. It is through this love that the Father begot the Son and that the Holy Spirit maintains the fellowship between Father and Son.

"God is love." These words are found twice in the fourth chapter of the first epistle of John (vv. 8, 16). What do they mean? I think they mean, first of all, that I must not seek love, for I may fail in doing so. If I want love, I must seek God, for love is the very nature of God. The Scripture does not say that God *has* love, but that God *is* love, and the love that I need is God Himself coming into my heart. Not a drop of pure, real, heavenly, everlasting love can come to us unless God is moved to give it as an act of His grace.

God has revealed His love in all of nature, even in the animals. Look at the way the little lamb clings to its mother and the way the mother sheep cares for the lamb. That is what we call love. Similarly, even among the most heathen and ungodly people, you can find love of a certain sort. But the love of heaven, the love of eternity, the love that will last, the love that is not in the flesh but that comes from heaven—that love is God. If I want that love, I must have God.

What a thought! Oh, let my heart bow in humble praise. I want this great God to come into me, to take possession of me, and to make me a vessel fit for His use (2 Tim. 2:21) so that He can fill me with love. Let the heart say, "Yes, my God, take me and fill me with love, for the sake of Your Son who died on Calvary."

The first question that arises here is, What do we need? We must know what we are seeking. Then our second question will be, What are we to do? What do we have to do to get what we are seeking? And the third question will be, What should we expect?

What Do We Need?

In Our Relationships with God

Look, first of all, at your relationship with God. Do you know the love of God as you ought to know it? Does it dwell upon you as an overshadowing power, the way the love of a mother dwells upon her child?

Do you know the love of God, and does it make you sing the song of the ransomed ones from morning to night? (See Isaiah 35:10.) There is not a heart that does not say, "Oh, I know the love of God too little." And why is that? It is because you have not been perfected in love. When the soul is perfected in love, it has such a sense of that love that it can rest in it for eternity; and though it has as much as it can contain for the time being, it can always receive more.

Again, are you not dissatisfied with your love for God? You sometimes think that you can say, "Oh, my God, I do love You." There are many Christians—real Christians—who do not say that. They are afraid to say it. They fear God; they say earnestly, "I wish to love God"; and they complain very honestly and bitterly, "Oh, my God, why do I have so little love?" But they hardly know what it is like to say, "Oh, God of heaven, how I love You! You know how my heart delights in You."

Have you not had to confess very often that you could not speak like that to God? And does there not arise in your heart a strong feeling of condemnation? You say, "Oh, my love for God is not what it should be!" And then sometimes, when you have a sense of God's love given to you for a moment in your fellowship with Him, is there not a cry, "Oh, why can it not abide with me"?

A child has no trouble rejoicing in his parents' love. I remember my little boy, when he was five or six, sometimes coming to the study door, opening it, and just looking in and smiling to see Papa's face. Then he would shut the door and go away happy. Or he would come on tiptoe just outside the window, looking in to see Papa, and then go off again to play. It was never an effort for the child to love the father.

Dear friend, God can do that for you. He can make His love cover you all day long, and your love will rise up to Him all day in deep restfulness and in childlike peace. I am sure God can do it. I am sure God wants to do it. This is what we need: more love, more of the love of God.

In Our Relationships with Others

What is it that we need? Look at our love for those around us, in our daily lives, in our families, with our husbands and wives, parents and children, brothers and sisters, employers and employees. Look at our daily lives in business. Look at our daily lives in society, with the people whom we meet. Remember the remarks that are so easily made about others. Think of the hasty judgments, the sharp words, the thoughtless expressions that escape our lips. Think of how many people there are on whom our eyes look without love going out toward them. Why is it such an effort to us, and why do we fall short?

I want you to get hold of one thought, and that is that love is the easiest and most natural thing in the world, the easiest and happiest thing in the world, as long as you have love in your heart. But if you do not have it, then you may try to love a little but will fail. Is God not able to take possession of the heart of His child? Is not God able, in His mighty power as God, to come into the heart of His child and to give His love and His Spirit? Is God not able to open a fountain of love, so that in all our daily conversation it will be love, love, love flowing out unceasingly? Is God not able? I believe He is, and you believe it, too.

Christ said, *"By this shall all men know that ye are my disciples, if ye have love one to another"* (John 13:35). But oh, the church of Christ has become known for its contentions and divisions. How terrible! Within the circle of the same little church, of the same little society, how often distrust and jealousy, unlovingness and harshness, arise among Christians! Dear friends, do you not feel that there is just one thing needed in your own homes and in your own circles and in your businesses? If your hearts were filled with God's love, how easy it would be to live to His glory!

In Our Work for God

And then there is one more thing. I must not only think of my relationship with God and my relationships with my fellowmen around me, but I must especially think of my work for God's kingdom.

What is it that is needed in the work of the church, and why do so many people complain of lack of power and lack of success? The one thing that is needed is the infinite love of God dwelling in us. What would that do for us? It would give us more than one thing. In the first place, it would give us a wonderful tenderness, gentleness, meekness, and humility in dealing with people.

What is the chief quality of Christ Jesus that makes Him so pleasing to the Father? It is His humility. Christ said, *"Learn of me; for I am meek and lowly in heart"* (Matt. 11:29). He made His way to the throne of glory in meekness and humility.

Tell me, is this not what is needed in our work for God? The spirit of tender compassion and of gentleness should be seen with every word we say about the people whose souls we are seeking; this is the sign of Christ's presence. And then, more love would not only make us gentle, but, as with Christ Himself, it would also be the power and the inspiration of a divine zeal that would cause us to sacrifice all.

If we loved others with the love of God, there would be much more power in our work, much more sacrifice of our time and our comfort in order to pray to God for souls, much more intercession. Oh, if we loved as we ought to love, how much more we would sacrifice our comfort! How often we would ask, "What more can we sacrifice for Jesus?"

If the love of God truly possessed us, we would sacrifice everything for souls. Our formality, our routine, our habits, the ways we have learned to walk—they would all pass away! Not only would we do more work, but we would also do different work, work breathed upon us by the love of God.

And then, when we have gotten the divine fire of Christ, the Lamb of God, the Spirit of the Lamb, who gave Himself to the cross, something will pass unconsciously and unwittingly out of us to others. They will not know what it is, and we will not know, but how many unconverted men will be converted by the power of God's love! Is this not what every worker needs?

It is the one thing the church needs, and—bless God—it is the one thing He wants to give us.

What Must We Do?

Suppose we truly see our need in our relationships with God, with society, and with the work we have to do for Christ. Then we ask, "What must we do?" The first thing is, there will have to be the discovery and confession of sin. We must not only confess our need, which is part of the process, but we must also go far deeper.

Use the words *perfect love* as if they were a lamp from heaven, and flash them first of all into your own heart and life. Look at your life in the light of that perfect love. Next, turn the light of those words, *perfect love,* onto Christ, to find out what is in Him and what He is able to do. Find out exactly what Christ can give you, what Christ can do for you, and how you can become possessed by the life and the love shown in Him for you. Then take this light, and turn it upon the face of the world, upon the work we have to do in our own immediate circles and among those who do not believe. Lastly, in the light of perfect love, go afresh to work for Jesus.

Discover Our Shortcomings

We must begin with ourselves, to let the light shine upon ourselves and upon our lives. And what does that mean? It means that within us there will have to be a distinct discovery of where we fail. I am not going to write down a list of transgressions against the law of love. But suppose we have discovered how far we have fallen short in thought and word and deed in the light of this perfect love. What then? Are we to come to God with these sins? Yes, and yet that is not enough. What we need is to find out what is the root of it all. And what is it?

I may have been a Christian for ten or twenty or thirty years, praying for God to give me love. But there is something that is like a devil within me so that I cannot love. What is this temper or this evil spirit? What is this coldness of disposition? God will lead us to see what is at the root of it. And what is it? Just one word: self.

When God created Adam, He gave him self-life. What was His purpose in doing so? It was so that Adam could bring that self-life to God to be filled with God's life. But Adam turned away from God and had that self-life closed against God. That is the corruption you and I have inherited from Adam: self. If grace comes into a Christian and begins to work in his heart, and if the seed of life is planted amid the mass of surrounding corruption, the Christian may strive and fight and pray and wrestle to conquer, but in vain!

Self is the one and only cause of his failure. He tries to pluck off a fruit here and a bud there; he cuts off one branch after another of this terrible enemy of love. He vows and strives and perhaps does grow a little in love, yet at the bottom there is no rest. Why? Because there is something there that will not love. Oh, may God reveal to us that terrible something: self. We will then understand that nothing less than death, the death to self, is what must occur if the love of God is to live in us. Therefore, the first step we have to take is to come to God and confess that there is something in us that must die and that we cannot slay.

Surrender Self to God

The next thing will be a fresh surrender to God. But oh, I think that with many it must be a different surrender than what they have made previously. Many people honestly surrender themselves to God, but they never understand what it means to surrender self. There is a great difference between surrendering yourselves and surrendering your self, as we use the word *self*. It means giving up your whole self as you are, that root out of which all the evil comes. Many people say, "Oh, yes, I want to give myself to God, just as I am, so that He may save me," but they have never yet understood what the self is that has to be given up and what it really means to give it up to God.

Yet God teaches the upright; He teaches him through deep humiliation, and then a man finds out, "I did indeed turn to God, and yet I never turned away from my self. I took myself, with my old will and temper, as I was, and gave myself to God, but that was not what God wanted. God wanted me to turn away from self." That is the surrender we must ask God to teach us; we must learn to give up this accursed self.

Dear friend, do you want to realize perfect love for God in this world? Does that self-will hinder you? You must find some way of dealing with that self, and you cannot deal with it yourself. It is only the love of God coming in that will cast out self; and before God will do that, self must be brought like a criminal, must be laid at His feet.

There is no cure for self but death. We must die to self. How can we do that? We cannot kill ourselves; we cannot be our own executioners. We cannot nail ourselves to the cross. God alone is the death of self. God Himself must do it. He allowed Christ to die on the cross, and then, when Christ had died, God raised Him up. That is why, when God brings a man to see all that there is in Christ and to receive Christ fully, the power of Christ's death can come upon him and he can die to sin; and if he dies to sin, he dies to self.

How can a man be dead to sin if he is not dead to self? Self is the very root of sin. There is no sin if there is no self. You can take away men's sins, and you can adorn the inner man until you think there is no sin there; but if self is there, sin is there also. Let us ask God to teach us what it is to have given up self. Let us then come and ask God for grace to give up ourselves to Him as we have never done before. Remember, *"God is love."*

Wait upon the Lord

Will you let Him come in? Will you surrender yourself to God? There is another thing that surrender to God implies. When you have come and surrendered yourself, you must then keep your place as one who is actually given into God's hands, in deep resignation, looking to Him for what He will do. Wait upon Him to quicken you and to make you alive from the dead. These are the three things you will need: confession, surrender, and faith. That faith is faith in the power of God, who raised Christ from the dead.

Christ Jesus was born in Bethlehem; in a similar manner, I am born by the Holy Spirit. But Christ Jesus had to be born again the second time. He had to be tried, tempted, and tested, developed and perfected, and then He had to give up His life. And out of the grave, when He was in hopeless, helpless, dark death, God raised Him up. That is what the Christian must come to.

Christ's birth in Bethlehem is the likeness of my new birth when I was converted. But the birth from the grave, when Christ became *"the firstborn from the dead"* (Col. 1:18), is the likeness and promise of that full birth in which the power of the death and life of Christ come into me, and in which I know what it is to be dead with Christ and risen with Him—dead to self and made alive unto God.

Let the one great thing that you do from the morning when you awake until the evening when you go to sleep be this: have trust in God. Trust Him for what He can do in making you partakers of Christ's death as the death to self. You will become partakers of His life as a life lived for God and in God, a life of perfect love. Say to God, "My Father, I trust in You, for what You alone can do," and say to yourself, "I am going to believe in God, in the mighty power with which He raised Christ from the dead to work in me and in God's children around me."

What Should We Expect?

Something Divine

Third, what should we expect? We know what we are seeking, and we know what we must do, but now comes the question, What should we expect? My answer is, Let us expect something beyond all expectation. We have so often limited God by our thoughts, and we are still doing it. Yet Paul spoke of *"love... which passeth knowledge"* (Eph. 3:19), and then he further said, "[God] *is able to do exceeding abundantly above all that we ask or think"* (v. 20). Now, prepare yourself for something that passes knowledge, for something that is above what you can think, and give God the honor of doing something divine.

Jesus Himself

Then, further, if you ask, "What must I expect?" I would sum it up in these words: Jesus Himself. The work of God the Father is to beget God the Son, and that is the work that goes on through eternity. When we talk about the concept of "eternal generation," this does not mean that it was a thing in the past. Eternity—what is eternity? Eternity is ever going on. It is an ever present *now,* and the one work of God the Father is to beget the Son.

The Indwelling Christ

What do I expect? I expect God to give the indwelling Christ to all the hearts that are prepared, in a power they have never known, so that they may be *"rooted and grounded in love"* (Eph. 3:17) and may know the *"love... which passeth knowledge"* (v. 19). That is what we need and what we may expect.

God has nothing for us but Jesus. God cannot give us anything beyond that, but He is willing and able to give the living Son born afresh into us. He reveals Him to us, and when the living Christ dwells in us, He will break open the fountain of love within us. That is what we need. Expect it now. Fix your eyes upon Jesus, Jesus Himself. He must do it. He has done it.

Christ has taught us that He gave up His life on Calvary so that, in His fellowship with us, our *"old man"* (Rom. 6:6) might be crucified with Him. He has done it all for us. We need God to reveal to us what that means and to make us partakers of it.

You may say, "I have so often tried to believe in Jesus, but there has been so much failure, and I am so ignorant." Paul prayed that God would strengthen believers mightily by the Holy Spirit. It is only the Father who can reveal the Son, and He does it only by the Holy Spirit. The doctrine of the Trinity is to many of us only a piece of our orthodoxy, a doctrine we read about in books, occasionally hear of in sermons, and confess on Sundays. Oh, concentrate on that prayer in Ephesians 3: God the Father giving the Holy Spirit to work mightily in us, and the Holy Spirit causing Jesus to dwell in us.

When Jesus dwells in us, then we are filled with love unto *"all the fulness of God"* (Eph. 3:19). We possess the triune God, not only in heaven, but also in our hearts. Fix your hearts upon this: the Father must do it, and what the Father must do, I must expect. The Father, God Almighty, will give this Jesus into my heart as an indwelling Savior. What the Father does is to strengthen us with might by the Holy Spirit in the inner man (Eph. 3:16). Expect that. Fix your heart upon God. That is the one way to the Father, and as you go along step-by-step, let your heart be filled with this: *"God is love."* Love is the divine omnipotence. Love is the life and the glory of God.

Yes, *"God is love."* There is the love of the Father, the love of the Son, and the love of the Spirit. Let us fix our hope on the love of the Father giving the Son into our hearts. Let us rejoice in the Son coming with God's perfect love to dwell within. Let us bow in stillness while the Holy Spirit works mightily within us to *"shed abroad"* (Rom. 5:5) the love. God will come to us and will bring us into His banqueting house, and His banner over us will be love (Song 2:4). May God teach the waiting heart to expect nothing less than His perfect love perfected in us.

6

Our Lord's Prayer

6

Our Lord's Prayer

✦━━✦━━✦

That the love wherewith thou hast loved
me may be in them, and I in them.
—John 17:26

If I want to find out the nature of perfect love, I must look to God's love for Christ. The above verse says, *"That the love wherewith thou hast loved me may be in them."* This was Christ's conclusion of His whole prayer in John 17. It was the whole purpose of His work. We can picture Christ saying, "That the love that I have tasted, that the love that rested on Me and dwells in Me, may now pass on to them." And so, if you want to know what the life of perfect love is, you must rise up to heaven itself and see the love that God has for Christ.

And if you ask how you can know what this perfect love in the Godhead is, I can only answer that the Father gave His own life to the Son; the Son was begotten of the Father, out of His bosom; and in the depths of the Godhead, Christ came forth from the Father. The eternal Word, who is God (John 1:1) and was *"in the beginning with God"* (v. 2), *"was made flesh"* (v. 14).

If God were not love, if He were anything that we could call selfish, He would not have a triune nature. Yet He could not be anything but triune. From eternity, God set His Son before Him as His image and His glory. When *"the Word was made flesh,"* God said, *"Thou art my Son; this day have I begotten thee"* (Ps. 2:7). When a man gives out his own life to another, that is love; and the love of God is that He gave all His life to His only Son, and He said that, for all eternity, He would never live without His Son.

The Only True Love

Here I learn the first lesson: love means a birth out of the heart of God. That is the only true love upon earth—love that will live and last through eternity. Even now it can only come out of the Godhead. It is the work of God to give that birth. Dear friends, as truly as Jesus Christ was born of God and was perfected in the Resurrection as *"the firstborn from the dead"* (Col. 1:18), you must be born of God in the power of the Resurrection, or you have no share in the love of God or the heaven of God.

Let us remember this. If we try to learn the lesson, I think God will teach us more and more that love means giving—and giving all. We sometimes give a little, but not all. To give all—that is love! What did the Father do for the Son? He made Him heir of all things. The Father let Christ share in everything. God gave Him a seat in His throne; He gave Him a place in the worship of the angels; by Him He created the world; and He gave Him all His glory and all His love. (See Hebrews 1:1–13.)

Do you want to know what love is? Oh, my heart cannot take it in, nor can my tongue express it; my thoughts cannot reach to all its fullness. Love means giving all. It is that way with God, and it is that way with us, too. If you are to have love, it means you are to give up everything to God—everything. God cannot be limited. With God, love means giving His life to His Son, and with that, giving everything. That is the love of God for Christ.

How did God prove His love for Christ? He gave Him His own life, He gave Him all things throughout the universe, and then He sent Him to die! You say, "That is strange; is that the love of God?" Yes, it is. You say, "Oh, that was an exception that became necessary, but it did not belong to the essence of God's love." No, it was not an exception. This sending His Son to die is the highest and most wonderful part of God's love for Christ. And how does it prove the love of God? I will tell you.

It was not possible in the nature of things for God to come to die upon earth for sinners, but God put the honor upon His Son when He said, "Go and become a man, and, in love, live the life of man and of humanity." It was the infinite love of the Father for the Son that made Him say, "I will put this honor upon My Son." God in His love sent Christ to die. We have heard in different ways that love always means death—the death of self. God sent Christ and said, "Go and obey My Word, and then lay down Your life to die for sin, to die to the world and self; give up Your life entirely for Me and My glory."

My friend, when you think of the love of God, has it ever said to you that you must die? The highest point of God's love is that He invites us to die utterly to self, to be like Himself and His Son, perfect in love. God's love for Christ means death. May we have grace to say, "I wish to enter into the death of Jesus; I wish to be nothing in myself, O my God! May Your love agree to accept me as nothing."

And then God raised Jesus from the dead. That also was the love of God, which led Christ in the path of death to the resurrection life, the resurrection glory, the eternal glory of heaven. If you want to learn the nature of love, remember these three things: love gave birth to the Son, love gave all to the Son, and love claimed all from the Son.

Oh, if we are to know perfect love, do not think this is too high for simple people. Do not say we cannot be troubled with theological doctrines about the relation of the Father to the Son. If we are to spend eternity with God, in fellowship with the Father and the Son, there is surely nothing of such absorbing interest for us as to know what is the relation of the Father and the Son, and what God's love is for Christ. God gave His Son to me, and with Him gave all. Love is God claiming everything. Only as I die can I enter into the new, the resurrection life; into perfect love; into the glory of God.

Christ's Love for Us

There is a second thought in this passage of Scripture. I must not only look at the love of the Father for Christ, but I must also look at the love of Christ for us.

How do I get that from our text? Very simply. Jesus prayed to the Father, *"That the love wherewith thou hast loved me may be in them."* What does that imply? Christ wants to share with us the love that God gave to Him, and He went to the Father and said, "Father, here are those whom I have redeemed. Father, I beg that they may have all the love that You have given Me and that it may rest in them." Is that not Christ's wonderful love? The Father took Christ up into a perfect likeness with Himself. As He had given everything to the Son in the depth of Godhead, He allowed the Son to show on earth what love is by giving everything back to the Father.

Christ also wants us to grow up into a perfect likeness with Himself. As God gave everything He had to Christ, so Christ gives everything He has to us, even the love of the Father. It was the love of Christ that prayed to the Father for us, so that the Father's love might come into us. What does this teach us? It reminds us of what Christ is doing in heaven. Christ, as a mighty King on the throne of God, prays day and night for us (Heb. 7:25). He gives up His life in glory to pray for us. He cannot die a second time, but just as He died on the cross on earth, He gives up His life in heaven to pray that the love of God may come down upon us. O friend, that is what love does.

Love That Prays

You say you want to know what love will do. Love will pray for others. It will say, just as Christ did, "I have this wonderful blessing of God's love, and I will give it to those around me." It should be our prayer: "Oh, let the love of God come down upon them also!" There is nothing that should make Christians as ashamed as their unappreciation of the influence of intercession for others. How many Christians have thought everything was right with them! They have spent their little time in prayer daily, their quarter hour or half hour, and they have benefited from it. Yet they have never made it a rule to make time to pray for others!

Have you ever set your heart upon the thought, "I can by much prayer bring down a blessing from heaven upon someone else"? Love calls on God. It comes to God as the fountain of love, and it has something to say. It gives its time and its ardent desire and says, "Father, I pray for a blessing on those around me!"

Jesus the King spends all His time in heaven praying. Do you believe it? It is true. We read in Hebrews that Christ *"ever liveth to make intercession for* [us]" (Heb. 7:25). And how much time do you spend in this loving activity? How little of this love we have! Father, forgive us. If you want to know what love is, look at the love of Christ praying for us.

Love That Labors

And then, just think further of what Jesus said in the rest of that prayer, of how He spoke of what He had done for those disciples: *"I have given them thy word"* (John 17:14). In the words that precede our text, He said, *"I have declared unto them thy name"* (v. 26). Love not only prays; love also works.

Christ had been working for three years upon those disciples. How patiently He had borne with them! How marvelously He had instructed them and led them step-by-step, humbling Himself to their weak capacities! Love not only prays, but it also teaches, it watches, and it labors. Remember, if we study this perfect love in the light of Christ's love, it means that we give up ourselves to pray for others and to work for others.

Love That Dies

One more thing: Christ not only prays and works, but He also dies. He said in John 17, "I sanctify Myself; I give Myself as a sacrifice for them that they may be sanctified." (See verse 19.)

Love dies for those whom it loves. You remember those solemn words in 1 John which say that Christ *"laid down his life for us: and we ought to lay down our lives for the brethren"* (1 John 3:16). There ought to be such love in us, we ought to so give our lives for others, that when it becomes needful, dying for them will be the natural result of our love. Love not only prays; love also labors. Love not only labors; love also dies. God's love is seen in that He gave Christ up to die as an honor and a privilege. Christ's love was seen in that He gave

His life. Perfect love gives its life for others. It is true in God, in Christ, and in ourselves.

Conditions for This Love

The third thought to which this verse leads us is the conditions on which this perfect love can be ours. For whom does Christ pray in this prayer? *"That the love wherewith thou hast loved me may be in them."* Is that for the whole world? No. For whom, then? Christ indicated certain qualities of those in whom He asked that God's love should dwell. These qualities are the required conditions if we are to receive this blessing of God's perfect love in our hearts.

Separation

What are these qualities? The first is separation from the world: *"They are not of the world, even as I am not of the world"* (John 17:14). Oh, Christian, if you want to know what perfect love is, you must come out of the world; you must be separate. You tell me, "I do not understand what that means." Never mind. Say to God, "Lord, I want to come out of the world; I want to live like a man who is not of this world but of the other world." The love of God cannot dwell in your heart if the spirit of the earth is there. It is impossible. It is only when you go out from the world that the love of God can enter into and take possession of you.

Obedience and Faith

Another quality is receiving the Word in obedience and faith. Christ said, *"I have given them thy word'* (John 17:14), they have received it, and they have believed that You have sent Me." That is another quality. The disciples forsook all to follow Christ, and they received His testimony and set their whole confidence upon it. That is what John set before us as the sign of perfect love: *"Whoso keepeth his word, in him verily is the love of God perfected"* (1 John 2:5).

Let me say this for your comfort: the love of these disciples for whom Christ prayed was very defective, and yet Christ accepted it as the obedience and the faith of loving hearts. And so, we can be sure that if we come to Christ with our feeble beginnings, He will receive our love and will daily lead us in the path of perfect love and perfect obedience—not the obedience of angels, but the perfect obedience of faith. That is the second condition of love.

Unity

The first condition is separation from the world, the second is obedience to God's Word, and the third is unity with believers around us. Christ prayed for this: *"That they may be one"* (John 17:11). God's children must acknowledge each other, wherever they meet, however they may differ in their church organizations or in other things. My brother must be as dear to me as Christ Jesus is. God's children must draw close together, or the gift of perfect love cannot come.

In the fellowship of love, Christians must prove to the world that there is something in them that is different from the world, that the Spirit of God and heaven, of perfect love, is in them. In the early church, there were many differences between Christians, but as long as they focused more on the things upon which they agreed than on those upon which they differed, the unity of love remained unbroken.

If the church of Christ had only continued to do that, how different our condition would be today! But we have been focusing too much on the things on which we differ, though many of these things are comparatively of little importance. Let us get hold of the thought that, just as we must be separate from the world and joined to Christ in obedience to His Word, so we must also be joined to each other.

My love for my brother is the only real test of my love for God and for Jesus. If we are to seek and to find the life of perfect love, if God's love for Christ is to be in us as He prayed it would be, then the condition must be fulfilled: we must give up ourselves to see that we always deal with God's children in love—unselfish, tender, self-sacrificing, ministering love.

Two Stages of the Christian Life

But in case some are discouraged by the fear that these conditions of the path to perfect love are beyond their reach, let me remind them of one thing. In Holy Scripture we find a great deal about two stages in the Christian life: the Old Testament and the New, a time of preparation and a time of fulfillment. The longer I study God's Word and the Christian life, the deeper my conviction grows that the difference between the Old and New Testaments is a radical one that runs not only through the life of the church, but also through the life of every believer.

Now, it was for His disciples that Christ prayed and asked, *"That the love wherewith thou hast loved me may be in them.*" It would seem that this was something that had not come yet. They did indeed love Jesus, but their love was an elementary, feeble love—the love of beginners.

Christ had said, *"If ye love me, keep my commandments"* (John 14:15). No doubt the disciples went away from that sacred hour fully intending to keep His Word, and yet how soon they forsook their Master! Christ saw that they did indeed love Him and longed to obey Him; He Himself said, *"The spirit indeed is willing, but the flesh is weak"* (Matt. 26:41). Christ saw their loving obedience, but they were still only in the preparatory stage; their best efforts were feeble. *"To will is present with me; but how to perform that which is good I find not"* (Rom. 7:18) was their experience.

And yet the disciples were on the sure path to perfect love. Christ was training them for something better. Amid all their failures, He saw their hearts were right with Him. Thank God for the comfort that this can give us.

There is another stage; this is what Christ prayed for. He seemed to say, "Father, there is a new time coming when You will pour down Your Holy Spirit upon them, when the love of God will fill them as it fills Me, when Your love in which I live will be in them as in Me, and I will be in them." Christ was praying for the Day of Pentecost. The three conditions necessary for the Day of Pentecost to come were found in them, so the Day of Pentecost came, and God's love filled them.

Our hearts may be saying honestly, "Perfect love, yes, perfect love—this is our constant plea," and yet we feel we have not attained it. Let us hold on to these three things in the Spirit: separation from the world, from its spirit and from its pleasures; acceptance of God's Word in faith and obedience; and unity with all God's children. Then Christ, who led His disciples on so wonderfully, will lead us on, too.

Love Perfected in Us

We now come to the fourth thought that our text verse suggests: the love of God perfected in us. This is what Christ prayed for: *"That the love wherewith thou hast loved me may be in them."* This refers to the Day of Pentecost. In John 14:20, Christ said, *"At that day ye shall know that I am in my Father...and I in you."* He also said, *"If ye love me, keep my commandments'* (v. 15), and the Father will love you" (v. 21).

A love for Christ was already in them. Yet there was also a love that they were still to obtain through the Holy Spirit. This they obtained at Pentecost, and we must have this if we wish to know perfect love. The question comes to us, What does it mean to have the love of the Father in us, the love with which the Father loved His Son? What does God aim to accomplish in us? *"That the love wherewith thou hast loved me may be in them"*!

A Love within Us

First of all, we must understand that the love of God is going to be within us. How is the love of God to be in us, possessing and ruling and filling our inmost beings? Just as thinking and feeling and willing are in us, and it is easy and natural for us to think and feel and will, even so, when the love of God really fills our hearts, love will flow out spontaneously and continuously. Instead of it being a duty, as it is in the earlier disciple stage, with its effort and failure, it becomes a delight. There is a love that cannot help loving, because God's love has been poured out and has taken complete possession of us.

Up to this time, the inward life of self has been continually getting the mastery. The love of self and of sin has been very deep in us. What Christ's prayer asks and promises is that we are now to have an inward life of love; in the place of sin and self, the love of God for Christ is now to fill the heart. Instead of us trying to love always and so often failing, love comes in as an indwelling divine power, constituting the very life of the soul, and helps us to love spontaneously, continuously, and most joyfully. Love has filled the heart. Think of this. My heart, my own heart, becomes the habitation of the holy love of God for Jesus in its divine joy and blessedness, its infinite power, its everlasting glory! *That the love wherewith thou hast loved me may be in them.* That love is to be our second nature, our new self, our very selves.

A Love through the Spirit

And then, note further, this love is to come through the Holy Spirit. Yes, the work of the Holy Spirit is this: in and through Him, the Father begets the Son. He is the love that is their living bond of union. You know it is a doctrine of the church that the Spirit proceeds from the Father and the Son. When Christ met the Father in glory after His resurrection, the Holy Spirit began to flow. The Father gave the Spirit to the Son, and the

Spirit flowed down from the Father through the Son to the disciples. It is this Holy Spirit who will now bring us the love of God as a heavenly reality, as a divine life, into our hearts. We have the Holy Spirit.

The disciples also had the Holy Spirit before the Day of Pentecost, but only as a secret power working in them. They did not know Him as a person. He had been given to live within them, but they did not know Him. They could not yet know Him as the One who brings the very love of Christ to them from the throne of God. In a similar manner, there are two stages in our experience. We struggle and wrestle and try and fight for love, but we don't succeed. Yet the words of our text give us the precious promise that gives us hope. As the Son prayed to the Father, *"That the love wherewith thou hast loved me may be in them,"* so we receive the blessed assurance that our hearts can be filled with the love of God in a way and to an extent that we have never known before, in the power of the Holy Spirit.

A Love Seen in Christ

Once more, if you want to know how this love of God is to be perfected in you, not only must you give your whole heart and wait for the Holy Spirit of God, but, above all things, you must also look to Jesus, through whom the Spirit comes and whom the Spirit will reveal. See how Christ connects the two things: *"That* [Your] *love…may be in them, and I in them"* (John 17:26). The indwelling love of God and the indwelling Son of God are inseparable.

Perhaps you cannot understand it, but the Son of God is the love of God. He was born of God's love; He was sent by God's love; He was raised from the dead by God's love; He dwells in the glory of God's love. Therefore, while we look for the Holy Spirit, let us set our hearts wide open and know that we can have within us a holy temple that can be filled with love, because Christ, who holds within Himself all God's love, comes to dwell there. Let us expect this with a trust and a confidence and a clinging to Christ, in whom the love of God is manifested. (See 1 John 4:9.) And as the prayer of Jesus brought Pentecost to the early disciples, so the prayer of Jesus brings Pentecost to the individual soul now. It is the intercession of Christ that can bring Pentecost and perfect the love of God in our hearts.

Two Questions

Let me ask you two simple questions. First, do you believe that this prayer can be fulfilled in you? Do you believe that it is God's will that the Holy Spirit should reveal His love for Jesus as a living reality and a continuous experience within your heart? I believe it! I believe it is God's will for you and for me. Perfect love is the love that is in God, that is in Christ, that is in the Holy Spirit for us so that He may bring it into our hearts. *"The fruit of the Spirit is love"* (Gal. 5:22).

Oh, look at the mystery of the love of the Father for Christ His Son, the love that fills eternity! Look at the love of the Son for us: heavenly love made manifest on earth. The love that the Spirit brings is this very same divine and heavenly love, and the Holy Spirit will pour out in our hearts this perfect, divine love (Rom. 5:5).

Let us fix our faith upon this. There is a perfect love for me, and the Holy Spirit is the messenger who will come and bring it through Jesus and from Jesus to me. Nothing short of this can satisfy the longing soul. I want it in my heart, and I may count upon it. Why? Because Jesus asked the Father that it would come. Have you set your heart upon that, and do you believe God means that it can come? The love with which the Father loved the Son is a divine, supernatural reality, a heavenly power that will dwell in and have possession of you.

Brother or sister, listen for a moment to the voice of Christ: "Father, You love Me, and I love them; according to the riches of Your glory, grant that the love with which You have loved Me may enter the hearts of My disciples and dwell there always, so that I can dwell there." Let us say, "Father, I believe it can be done!"

And then my second question is, If you believe it can be done, are you going to yield yourself to it? Love claims all. Love is very exacting. God asked Christ to give His life up to Him, and He could not do anything else. Likewise, Christ asks His disciples to forsake everything for Him. Christ asks us to be ready to give up our lives for others. Perfect love needs a perfect heart, perfectly given up to love alone. It asks that we yield ourselves and say, "Lord, here I am, and I part with everything in the world so that love may have possession of every word I speak and every thought I have and every act I do. I want every moment of my life to be a sacrifice to Your love, so that nothing but love can come out of me!"

Are you afraid to speak these words? Do you feel as if you do not dare to pray them, because you do not know how it can come about? It must come as a divine, supernatural gift, as the power of God. It is not a thing that can be attained, reached, or grasped. But are you willing to surrender yourself to be like Christ, nothing but a servant of divine love?

It is a very solemn thing that, on the Day of Judgment, our love for God is going to be tried by our love for man and our treatment of our fellowman. We have to be judged by the test of love. Remember that. You are not going to get into heaven by *"faith without works"* (James 2:20), but by faith and works of love. (See verses 14–26.) You are pardoned by faith without one good work (see Romans 3:28; 5:1), but in the Day of Judgment, good deeds will be taken into account. (See Matthew 16:27; 26:32–46.)

Remember every day as you come to God that God judges your love for Him by your conduct toward your fellowman. What did John tell us?

Let us not love in word, neither in tongue; but in deed and in truth. And hereby we know that we are of the truth, and shall assure our hearts before [God].   (1 John 3:18–19)

"He that loveth not his brother whom he hath seen, how can he love God whom he hath not seen?" (1 John 4:20). Your love for God is imagined, a sentiment, a delusion, if your heart is not full of love for your fellowman.

Oh, friend, this perfect love comes as a very solemn claim, with its demand on every moment of our lives that the world around may see that it is real. Are you willing to give up your life to it? I am not going to ask just now if you have attained it. However, are you willing to submit to God, so that the love with which God loved Christ, the love that sent Him to die for men, may have you wholly for itself? God wants us to say, "My God, I give myself up to live only, always, and wholly for Your love." You feel it is impossible; you feel utterly helpless; you cannot undertake to live this life of perfect love. But do not be afraid; the more helpless you are, the better.

We need to sink right down into despair. It was after Christ was dead and in the grave that God raised Him up to glory. You must sink down into death and utter helplessness and say, "My God, I want love, and my love is passing away from me. Oh, be my support!" You must sink down into the grave of your own powerlessness, the grave of self, and let God Himself lift you up! If only you are willing to acknowledge God's claim and to say, "My Father, here I am. This love with which You loved Your Son is too high for me—beyond my reach. But if You will hear His prayer, here I am; let that love enter and take possession of me. I yield myself to its blessed power—let it live in me!"

Will you claim this? Will you accept this? I know it is not an easy thing.

You think, perhaps, that you are not prepared for it; but come, come now before God. Do you really believe that the words of this prayer can be fulfilled in your spirit? Is it possible? Can you say your *"yea"* and *"Amen"* (2 Cor. 1:20) to God? And then, are you willing to absolutely surrender your whole life, to wait every day upon God for His power and love to maintain within you the life of perfect love, the life of God's love for Christ living in you?

Are you ready now in faith to believe in the mighty power of the Holy Spirit to bring the full answer to the prayer, *"That the love wherewith thou hast loved me may be in them, and I in them"*? Are you ready to believe that God will grant what is written in His Word: love perfected in us, we perfected in love? God holds out the promise. The mighty, all-prevailing intercession of Christ pleads for it. The Holy Spirit can and will bring it about. The triune God is my surety for it. Lord, I do believe! Grant it for Your name's sake. Amen.

7

Privilege and Experience

7

Privilege and Experience

And he said unto him, Son, thou art ever
with me, and all that I have is thine.
—Luke 15:31

The words of the above Scripture are
familiar to us all. The elder son had complained and said that though his father
had made a feast and had killed the fatted calf
for the Prodigal Son, he had never given him
even a young goat so that he might be merry
with his friends. The answer of the father was,
"Son, thou art ever with me, and all that I have is
thine."

We cannot have a more wonderful revelation of the heart of our Father in heaven than

what this points out to us. We often speak of how the father's heart was revealed in his welcome to the Prodigal Son and in what he did for him. But we also have a far more wonderful revelation of the father's love in what he said to the elder son.

If we are to experience a deepening of the spiritual life, we need, on the one hand, to discover clearly what is the spiritual life that God wants us to live. On the other hand, we need to ask whether we are living that life, or, if we are not, what hinders us from living it out fully. This subject naturally divides itself into these categories:

1. The high privilege of every child of God.

2. The low experience of too many believers.

3. The cause of the discrepancy.

4. The way to the restoration of the privilege.

Our High Privilege

Our text verse contains two things that describe the privilege that every child of God has. First, *"Son, thou art ever with me."* This implies that unbroken fellowship with the Father is our portion. Second, *"All that I have is thine."* This means that everything that God can bestow upon His children is theirs. We can hear God saying, *"'Thou art ever with me'*; I am always near you; you can dwell every hour of your life in My presence, and all I have is for you. I am a father, with a loving father's heart. I will withhold nothing good from you." In these promises, we have the rich privileges of God's heritage.

Unbroken Fellowship

We have, in the first place, unbroken fellowship with Him. A father never sends his child away without caring whether his child knows that he loves him. The father longs to have his child believe that he has the light of his father's countenance upon him throughout the day—that, if he sends him away to school or to anywhere else, it is with a sense of sacrifice to his parental feelings. If this is so with an earthly father, how must it be with God? Does He not want every child of His to know that he is constantly living in the light of His countenance? This is the meaning of that statement, *"Son, thou art ever with me."*

That was the privilege of God's people in Old Testament times. We are told that *"Enoch walked with God"* (Gen. 5:22). God's promise to Jacob was,

> *Behold, I am with thee, and will keep thee in all places whither thou goest, and will bring thee again into this land; for I will not leave thee, until I have done that which I have spoken to thee of.*　(Gen. 28:15)

God's promise to Israel through Moses was, *"My presence shall go with thee, and I will give thee rest"* (Exod. 33:14). In Moses' response to the promise, he said,

> *For wherein shall it be known here that I and thy people have found grace in thy sight? is it not in that thou goest with us? so shall we be separated, I and thy people, from all the people that are upon the face of the earth.*　(v. 16)

The presence of God with Israel was the mark of their separation from other people. This is the truth taught in all the Old Testament. How much more may we look for it in the New Testament! Thus we find our Savior promising to those who love Him and who keep His Word, that the Father also will love them, and Father and Son will come and make their abode with them (John 14:23).

Let this thought into your hearts, that every child of God is called to this blessed privilege, to live every moment of his life in fellowship with God. He is called to enjoy the full light of God's countenance. There are many Christians—I suppose the majority of Christians—who seem to think that the Spirit's work is only to convict and convert. They hardly know that He came to dwell in our hearts and there to reveal God to us. He did not come to dwell near us, but in us, so that we might be filled with His indwelling.

We are commanded to *"be filled with the Spirit"* (Eph. 5:18). When we are filled with the Spirit, He makes God's presence manifest to us. That is the whole teaching of the epistle to the Hebrews: the veil is torn in two; we have access into the Holy of Holies by the blood of Jesus; we come into the very presence of God so that we can live all day with that presence resting upon us. That presence is with us wherever we go; and in all kinds of trouble, we have undisturbed repose and peace. *"Son, thou art ever with me."*

There are some people who seem to think that God, by some unintelligible sovereignty, withdraws His face from them. But God loves His people too much to withhold His fellowship from them without reason. The true reason of the absence of God from us is to be found in our sin and unbelief, rather than in any sovereignty of His. If a child of God is walking in faith and obedience, he will enjoy the divine presence in unbroken continuity.

Sharing in His Gifts

Then there is the next blessed privilege: *"All that I have is thine."* Thank God, He has given us His own Son; and in giving Him, He has given us all things that are in Him. He has given us Christ's life, His love, His Spirit, His glory. *"All things are yours....And ye are Christ's; and Christ is God's"* (1 Cor. 3:21, 23).

God bestows upon every one of His children all the riches of His Son, the everlasting King. *"Son, thou art ever with me, and all that I have is thine."* Is that not the meaning of all those wonderful promises given in connection with prayer, such as, *"And whatsoever ye shall ask in my name, that will I do"* (John 14:13)? Yes, there it is. That is the life of the children of God, as He Himself has pictured it to us.

Our Low Experience

Now, in contrast with this high privilege of believers, let us look at the low lives that so many of us live. The elder son was living with his father and serving him *"these many years"* (Luke 15:29), and he complained that the father never gave him a young goat, while he gave his prodigal brother the fatted calf.

Why was this? Simply because he did not ask for it. He did not believe that he would get it, and therefore he never asked for it and never enjoyed it. He thus continued to live in constant murmuring and dissatisfaction, and the keynote of this wretched life is provided in what he said. His father gave him everything, yet he never enjoyed it; and he threw the whole blame on his loving and kind father.

Oh, beloved, is this not the life of many believers? Do not many of them speak and act in this way? Every believer has the promise of unbroken fellowship with God, but some will still say, "I have not enjoyed it; I have tried hard and done my best, and I have prayed for the blessing, but I suppose God does not see fit to grant it to me."

But why not? One says it is the sovereignty of God withholding the blessing. But the father in the parable did not withhold his gifts from the elder brother because of sovereignty, nor does our heavenly Father withhold any good thing from those who love Him (Ps. 84:11). He does not make any such distinctions among His children. *"God is able to make all grace abound toward you"* (2 Cor. 9:8) was a promise made equally to everyone in the Corinthian church.

Others think these rich blessings are not for them but for those who have more time to devote to religion and prayer. Or they think that their circumstances are so difficult, so peculiar, that we can have no conception of their various hindrances. But do such people think that God, if He places them in these circumstances, cannot make His grace abound accordingly? They admit He could work a miracle for them if He wanted to, which they can hardly expect.

In some ways, they, like the elder son, throw the blame on God. Thus, when asked if they are enjoying unbroken fellowship with God, many are saying, "No, I have not been able to reach such a height; it is too high for me. I know of some who have it, and I read of it, but God has not given it to me for some reason."

But why not? Perhaps you think that you do not have the same capacity for spiritual blessing that others have. The Bible speaks of a joy that is *"unspeakable and full of glory"* (1 Pet. 1:8), like the fruit of believing; of a *"love of God...shed abroad in our hearts by the Holy Ghost which is given unto us"* (Rom. 5:5). Do we enjoy these blessings? If not, why? We desire them; why do we not get them? Have we asked for them? We think we are not worthy of the blessings; we think we are not good enough, and that therefore God has not given them. But there are more people among us than we know of, or are willing to admit, who throw the blame of our darkness and of our wanderings on God. Take care not to do this!

Again, the Father says, *"All that I have is thine."* Are you rejoicing in the treasures of Christ? Are you conscious of having an abundant supply for all your spiritual needs every day? God has all these for you in abundance. You might complain to Him, "You never gave me a young goat!" (Luke 15:29). But His answer always is, *"'All that I have is thine.'* I gave it to you in Christ."

Dear reader, we have such wrong thoughts about God. What is God like? I know no image more beautiful and instructive than that of the sun. The sun is never weary of shining, of pouring out its beneficent rays upon both the good and the evil. (See Matthew 5:45.) You might close up the windows with blinds or bricks, but the sun will shine upon them just the same; though we might sit in darkness, in utter darkness, the shining would be the same. God's sun shines on every leaf, on every flower, on every blade of grass, on everything that springs out of the ground. Everything receives this wealth of sunshine until it grows to perfection and bears fruit.

Would He who made that sun be less willing to pour out His love and life into me? The sun—what beauty it creates! And my God—would He not delight more in creating a beauty and a fruitfulness in me, as He has promised to give? And yet some say, when asked why they do not live in unbroken communion with God, "God does not give it to me; I do not know why. But that is the only reason I can give you—He has not given it to me."

Remember the parable of the one who said, *"I knew thee that thou art an hard man, reaping where thou hast not sown, and gathering where thou hast not strowed'* (Matt. 25:24), asking and demanding what you have not given." This is how some people picture God. Oh, let us come and ask why believers have such a low experience!

The Cause of This Discrepancy

The believer complains that God has never given him a young goat, or that God has given him some blessing but has never given the full blessing. He has never filled him with His Spirit. "I never," he says, "had my heart, as a fountain, giving forth the rivers of living waters promised in John 7:38." What is the cause of this?

The elder son thought he was serving his father faithfully for many years, but it was in the spirit of bondage and not in the spirit of a child. Therefore, his unbelief blinded him to the idea of a father's love and kindness. He was unable all the time to see that his father was ready to give him not only a young goat, but even a hundred or a thousand of them, if he wanted them. He was simply living in unbelief, in ignorance, in blindness, robbing himself of the privileges that the father had for him.

So, if there is a discrepancy between our lives and the fulfillment and enjoyment of all God's promises, the fault is ours. If our experience is not what God wants it to be, it is because of our unbelief in the love of God, in the power of God, and in the reality of God's promises.

God's Word teaches us, in the story of the Israelites, that it was unbelief on their part that caused their troubles, not any limitation or restriction on God's part. As Psalm 78 says,

> *He clave the rocks in the wilderness, and gave them drink as out of the great depths. He brought streams also out of the rock, and caused waters to run down like rivers.*
>
> (vv. 15–16)

Yet Israel sinned by doubting His power to provide meat for them. *"Yea, they spake against God; they said, Can God furnish a table in the wilderness?"* (v. 19).

Later on, we read in verse forty-one, *"They turned back and tempted God, and limited the Holy One of Israel."* They kept distrusting Him from time to time. When they got to Kadesh-Barnea and God told them to enter the land flowing with milk and honey, where they would find rest, abundance, and victory, only two men said, "Yes, we can take possession, for God can make us conquer." (See Numbers 13:30.) But the ten spies and the six hundred thousand men answered, "No, we can never take the land; the enemies are too strong for us." (See verse 31.) It was simply unbelief that kept them out of the Land of Promise.

If there is to be any deepening of the spiritual life in us, we must come to discover and acknowledge the unbelief that is in our hearts. God grant that we may get this spiritual quickening. May we come to see that, by our unbelief, we have prevented God from doing His work in us.

Unbelief is the mother of disobedience and all other sins and shortcomings: our tempers, our pride, our unlovingness, our worldliness, our sins of every kind. Though these differ in nature and form, they all come from the one root, namely, that we do not believe in the freedom and fullness of the divine gift of the Holy Spirit to dwell in us, to strengthen us, and to fill us with the life and grace of God all day long. I ask you to look at the elder son and ask what was the cause of that terrible difference between the heart of the father and the experience of the son. There can be no answer but that it was this sinful unbelief that utterly blinded the son to a sense of his father's love.

Dear fellow believer, if you are not living in the joy of God's salvation, the entire cause is your unbelief. You do not believe in the mighty power of God, that He is willing, by His Holy Spirit, to bring about a thorough change in your life and enable you to live in fullness of consecration to Him. God wants you to live in this way, but you do not believe it. If men really believed in the infinite love of God, what a change it would bring about!

What is love? It is a desire to communicate oneself for the good of the object loved; it is the opposite of selfishness, as we read in 1 Corinthians 13:5: "[Love] *seeketh not her own.*" Just as a mother is willing to sacrifice herself for the good of her child, so God in His love is ever willing to impart blessing. He is omnipotent in His love. This is true, my friends: God is omnipotent in love, and He is doing His utmost to fill every heart who comes to Him. You ask, "But if God is really anxious to do that, and if He is almighty, why does He not just do it now?" You must remember that God has given you a will, and by the exercise of that will, you can hinder God and remain content, as the elder son was, with the low life of unbelief.

We have now seen the cause of the difference between God's high, blessed provision for His children and the low, sad experience of many of us in the unbelief that distrusts and grieves Him. Let us ask how we can be brought to live up to our privileges.

The Way of Restoration

We all know the parable of the Prodigal Son. From that parable, many sermons have been preached about repentance. We are told that he said to himself, *"I will arise and go to my father, and will say unto him, Father, I have sinned against heaven, and before thee"* (Luke 15:18). Preachers speak of this as the first step in a changed life—as conversion, repentance, confession, or returning to God. But because this was the first step for the Prodigal, we must remember that this is also the step to be taken by His erring children, by all *"which* [think they] *need no repentance"* (v. 7).

Those Christians who do not understand how wrong their low religious lives are must be taught that unbelief is sin. They must come to see that it is as necessary that they be brought to repentance as it was for the Prodigal. You have heard a great deal of preaching to the unconverted about repentance, but I am preaching it to God's children. We have a picture of so many of God's children in that elder brother. What the father told the elder brother, to bring him to a sense of the love that he had for him, just as he loved the prodigal brother, was meant to unveil to the elder brother the evil disposition that was in him.

Likewise, God tells each of us in our contentedness with our low lives, "You must repent and believe that I love you, and that all that I have is yours. By your unbelief, you have dishonored Me, living for ten, twenty, or thirty years as a Christian, but never believing what it was to live in the blessedness of My love. You must confess the wrong you have done to Me in this and be broken down in contrition of heart just as truly as the Prodigal was."

There are many children of God who need to confess that, although they are His children, they have never believed that God's promises are true and that He is willing to fill their hearts all day long with His blessed presence. Have you believed this? If you have not, all my teaching will be of no profit to you.

Will you not say, "By the help of God, I will now begin a life of faith and will not rest until I know what such a life means. I will believe that I am every moment in the Father's presence and that all He has is mine"?

May the Lord God work this conviction in the hearts of all feeble believers! Have you ever heard the expression, "a conviction for sanctification"? You know that the unconverted man needs conviction before conversion. In the same way, the carnally-minded Christian needs conviction before he comes to a real insight of spiritual blessedness. To be sanctified, he must be convicted a second time because of his sinful life of doubt, temper, and unlovingness. He must be broken down under that conviction; then there is hope for him. May the Father of Mercy grant all such individuals that deep contrition, so that they may be led into the blessedness of His presence and enjoy the fullness of His power and love!

8

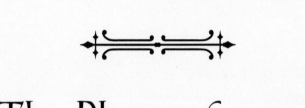

The Blessing Secured

8

The Blessing Secured

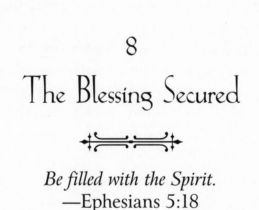

Be filled with the Spirit.
—Ephesians 5:18

If I have only a little air in my lungs, that will not be enough for me to keep up a healthy, vigorous life. Everyone needs to have his lungs well-filled with air, and the benefit of this can be felt in his blood and through his whole being. Similarly, the Word of God comes to us and says, "Christians, do not be content with thinking that you have the Spirit, or with having a little of the Spirit; but if you want to have a healthy life, *'be filled with the Spirit.'*"

Do you have this Spirit-filled life? Or are you ready to cry out, "Oh, I do not know what it is like to be filled with the Spirit, but it is what I desire!" If this is your heart's cry, I want to point out to you the path by which you may come to this great, precious blessing that is meant for every one of us.

Before I go into more detail, let me just note one misunderstanding that prevails. People often look upon being *"filled with the Spirit"* as something that comes with a mighty stirring of the emotions, a sort of heavenly glory that comes over them, something that they can feel strongly and mightily; but that is not always the case.

I was recently at Niagara Falls. I noticed, and I was told, that the water was unusually low. Suppose the river were doubly full. How would you see that fullness in the Falls? You would see it in the increased volume of water pouring over the waterfall, and you would hear it in its tremendous noise. But go to another part of the river, or to the lake, where the very same fullness is found, and there is perfect quiet and placidity; the rise of the water is gentle and gradual, and you can hardly notice that there is any disturbance as the lake gets full.

And so it may be with a child of God. To one the Spirit comes with mighty emotion and with a blessed awareness that, "God has touched me!" To others it comes in a gentle filling of the whole being with the presence and the power of God by His Spirit. I do not want to determine the way in which it will come to you, but I want you simply to take your place before God and say, "My Father, whatever it may mean, that is what I want." If you come and give yourself up as an empty vessel and trust God to fill you, God will do His own work.

And now, I will note four steps by which a man can attain this wonderful blessing of being *"filled with the Spirit."* He must say, first of all, "I *must* have it." Then he must say, "I *may* have it." Third, he must say, "I *will* have it." And then, last, "Thank God, I *shall* have it."

A Command for All Christians

The first thing a man must begin to say is, "I *must* have it." He must feel, "It is a command of God, and I cannot live unfilled with the Spirit without disobeying God." It is a command here in our text: *"And be not drunk with wine...but be filled with the Spirit"* (Eph. 5:18). God wants it for each of His children. Oh, that everyone might be brought to say, "If

I am to please God, I must *'be filled with the Spirit'*!

I fear there is a terrible, terrible self-satisfaction among many Christians. They are content with their low level of life. They think they have the Spirit because they are converted, but they know very little of the joy and sanctifying power of the Holy Spirit. They know very little of the fellowship of the Spirit linking them to God and to Jesus. They know very little of the power of the Spirit to testify for God, and yet they are content and will often say, "Oh, such things are only for the strongest of Christians."

My niece once said to me as I was talking to her, "Oh, Uncle Andrew, I cannot try to make myself better than the Christians around me. Wouldn't that be presumptuous?" And I said, "My child, you must not ask what the Christians around you are, but you must be guided by what God says." She has since confessed to me how bitterly ashamed she has become of what she asked me and how she went to God to seek His blessing. Oh, friends, do not be content with that half-Christian life that many of you are living, but say, "God wants it; God commands it; I must be *'filled with the Spirit.'*"

And you should look not only at God's command, but also at the need of your own soul. If you are a parent and you want your children to be blessed and converted, you may complain that you do not have the power to bless them. You say, "My home must be filled with God's Spirit." You complain of your own soul, of times of darkness and of leanness; you complain of your watchfulness and wandering.

A young minister once said to me, "Oh, why is it I have such a delight in study and so little delight in prayer?" My answer was, "My brother, your heart must get filled with a love for God and Jesus, and then you will delight in prayer."

You complain sometimes that you cannot pray. There is so little joy in prayer; you do not know what to pray; something always drags you away from your prayer closet. It is because you are trying to live a holy life, trying to live a life well-pleasing to God, without being *"filled with the Spirit."*

Oh, think of the needs of the church around you! You may be a Sunday school teacher who is trying to teach a class of ten or twelve children, and perhaps not even one of them is converted. They go out from your class unconverted because you are trying to do a heavenly work in the power of the flesh. Sunday school teachers, do begin to say, "I must be filled with the Spirit of God, or I must give up the responsibility for these young souls; I cannot teach them."

Or think of the need of the world. If you were to send out missionaries full of the Holy Spirit, what a blessing that would be! Why is it that many missionaries complain in the foreign field, "It was there that I learned how weak and how unfit I am"? It is because the churches from which they go are not filled with the Holy Spirit.

Someone said to me in England a few weeks ago, "They talk so much about the volunteer movement and more missionaries, but we need something else; we need missionaries who are filled with the Holy Spirit." If the church is to get right with God, and the mission field is to get right, we must each begin with himself. It must begin with you. Begin with yourself and say, "O God, for Your sake; O God, for Your church's sake; O God, for the sake of the world, help me! I must be filled with the Holy Spirit."

What foolishness it would be for a man who had lost a lung and a half, and had hardly a quarter of a lung to do the work of two, to expect to be a strong man, to do hard work, and to live in any climate. What foolishness for a man to expect to live—when God has told him he cannot do so—a full Christian life unless he is full of the Holy Spirit! And what foolishness for a man who has only a little drop of the river of the water of life to expect to live and to have power with God and man! Jesus wants us to come and receive the fulfillment of the promise, *"He that believeth on me...out of his belly shall flow rivers of living water"* (John 7:38).

Oh, begin to say, "If I am to live a right life, if I am in every part of my daily life and conduct to glorify my God, I must have the Holy Spirit. I must be *'filled with the Spirit.'"* Are you going to say that? Talking about it for months and months won't help. Do submit to God, and as an act of submission say, "Lord, I confess it; I ought to be filled; I must be filled. Help me!" And God will help you.

Our Privilege of Being Filled

Then comes the second step: "I *may* be filled." The first had reference to duty; the second has reference to privilege: "I may be filled." Unfortunately, so many people have grown so accustomed to their low condition that they do not believe that they may, they can, actually be filled. And what right do I have to say that you ought to speak these words?

My right is this: God wants healthy children. Today I saw a six-month-old child, as beautiful and chubby as you could wish a child to be. With what delight the father and the mother looked upon him, and what a joy it was to see such a picture of health! Oh, do you think that God in heaven does not care for His children, and that God wants some of His children to live sickly lives? I tell you, it is not true! God wants every child of His to be a healthy Christian.

But you cannot be a healthy Christian unless you are filled with God's Spirit. Beloved, we have grown accustomed to a style of life. We see good Christians—as we call them—earnest men and women, full of failings, and we think, "Well, that is human. That man loses his temper, and that man is not as kind as he should be, and that man's word cannot always be trusted as ought to be the case, but...."

In daily life we look upon Christians and think, "Well, if they are faithful in going to church and in giving to God's cause, in attending the prayer meeting and in having family prayers; if they are fairly consistent, we thank God for them and say, 'We wish there were more people like them.'" But we forget to ask, "What does God want?" Oh, that we might see that this blessing is meant for each one of us!

My brother, my sister, there is a God in heaven who has been longing for these past years, while you never thought about it, to fill you with the Holy Spirit. God longs to give the fullness of the Spirit to every child of His.

The letter to the Ephesians was written to poor heathens, only recently brought out from heathendom. They were a people among whom there was still stealing and lying, for they had only just come into Christianity. But Paul said to every one of them, *"Be filled with the Spirit."* God is ready to do it; God wants to do it. Oh, do not listen to the temptation of the Devil when he says, "This is only meant for some eminent people, for the strongest Christians who have a great deal of free time to devote to prayer and to seeking after it, for those who have a receptive temperament— those people can be filled with the Spirit."

Who can dare say, "I cannot be filled with the Spirit"? Who will dare to say that? If any of you speak in this way, it is because you are unwilling to give up sin.

Do not think that you cannot be filled with the Spirit because God is not willing to give it to you. Did the Lord Jesus not promise the Spirit? Is the Holy Spirit not the best part of His salvation? Do you think He gives half a salvation to any of His redeemed ones? Is His promise not for all, *"He that believeth on me...out of his belly shall flow rivers of living water"* (John 7:38)?

This is more than fullness—this is over-flow—and this is what Jesus has promised to everyone who believes in Him. Cast aside your fears, your doubts, and your hesitation, and say at once, "I can be filled with the Spirit; I may be filled with the Spirit. There is nothing in heaven or earth or hell that can prevent it, because God has promised, and God is waiting to do it for me." Are you ready to say, "I may; I can; I can be filled with the Spirit, for God has promised it, and God will give it"?

Having the Will

And so we come to the third step, when a man says, "I *will* have it!" He begins with, "I must have it" and "I may have it," and now he says, "I *will* have it." You know what it means when a man says in everyday matters, "I will have it." He goes and does everything that is to be done to get possession of it.

Very often a man wants to buy something, and he wishes for it, but wishing is not willing. I may want to buy a horse, and a man is asking five hundred dollars for it, but I do not want to pay more than four hundred dollars. I wish for it, I wish it very much, so I go and say to the man, "Give me the horse for the four hundred dollars." And he will say, "No, five hundred dollars." I love the horse, it is just what I want, but I am not willing to give the price. At last he says, "Well, you must give me an answer; I can get another purchaser," and I answer, "No, I won't have it. I want it very much; I long for it, but I won't give the price. I will not have it."

Give Up Sin

Dear friends, are you going to say, "I will have this blessing"? What does that mean? It means, first of all, of course, that you are going to give up every sin. You need to look into your life, and if you see anything wrong there, it means that you must confess it to

Jesus and say, "Lord, I cast it at Your feet. It may be rooted in my heart, but I will give it up to You. I cannot take it out, but Jesus, the Cleanser of sin, I give it to You." It does not matter if it is your temper, pride, greed, lust, pleasure, the fear of man, or anything else; give it up and say to Christ at once, "I will have this blessing at any cost." Oh, give up every sin to Jesus!

Give Up Self

And it not only means giving up every sin, but also giving up what is deeper than sin and more difficult to get at: it means giving up your self. You must give up self, with your will, your pleasure, your honor, and all you have, saying, "Jesus, I am from this moment going to give myself up, so that by Your Holy Spirit You may take possession of me, and so that You may by Your Spirit take out whatever is sinful and take entire command of me."

This looks difficult as long as Satan blinds us and makes us think it would be a hard thing to give up all that. But if God opens our eyes for one minute to see what a heavenly blessedness and what heavenly riches and heavenly glory it is to be filled with the Spirit out of the heart of Jesus, then we will say, "It may cost me anything, anything at all, but I will have the blessing." It means that you are just to cast yourself at His feet and to say, "Lord, I will have the blessing."

Ah, Satan often tempts us and says, "Suppose God were to ask that of you; would you be willing to give it?" and he makes us afraid. But so many have found, and have been able to tell about it, that once they have said, "Lord, anything and everything!" the light and the joy of heaven have filled their hearts.

One afternoon last year in Johannesburg, South Africa, we had a testimony meeting, and a woman rose up and told us how her pastor two months before had held a consecration service in a tent. He had spoken strongly about consecration and had said, "Now, if God were to send your husband away to China, or if God were to ask you to go away to America, would you be willing to do it? You must give yourself up entirely." At the close of the meeting, the pastor had asked those to rise who were willing to give up all to be filled with the Spirit. The woman recalled—and her face beamed with brightness when she spoke— how she had said to herself, "God may take away my husband or my children from me. Am I ready for it? Oh, Jesus is very precious, but I cannot say I will give up all. But I will tell Him I do want to do it." The struggle was terrible, but at last she stood up.

She said she went home that night in a terrible struggle, and she could not sleep, for the thought running through her mind was, "I said to Jesus *everything,* but could I give up my husband or my child?" The struggle continued until midnight. "But," she said, "I could not let go. At last I said to Jesus, 'You can have everything, but fill me with Yourself.'" And the joy of the Holy Spirit came down upon her. Her pastor told me afterward that the testimony was a true one, and for the past two months her life had been one of exceeding brightness and heavenly joy.

Are you, my reader, tempted to say, "I cannot give up all"? I take you by the hand, my brother, my sister; I bring you to the crucified Jesus, and I say, "Just look at Him, how He loved you on Calvary; just look at Him." Just look at Jesus! He offers to actually fill your heart with His Holy Spirit, with the Spirit of His love, of His fullness, and of His power, to actually make your heart full of the Holy Spirit. Do you dare to say, "I am afraid"? Do you dare to say, "I cannot do that for Jesus"? Will your heart not cry out at His feet, "Lord Jesus, anything, but I must be filled with Your Spirit"?

Haven't you often prayed for the presence, the abiding nearness, and the love of Jesus to fill you? But that cannot happen until you are filled with the Holy Spirit. Oh, come and say, in view of any sacrifice, "I will have it, with God's help! Not in my strength, but with the help of God, I will have it!"

Receiving the Blessing

And then comes the last step. Say, "I *shall* have it." Praise God that a man dares to say, "I shall have it." Yes, when a man has made up his mind; when a man has been brought to a conviction and a sorrow for his sinful life; when a man, like Peter, has wept bitterly or has sighed deeply before God, "Oh, my Lord, what a life I have been living!"; when a man has felt wretched in the thought, "I am not living the better life, the Jesus life, the Spirit life"; when a man begins to feel that, and when he comes and surrenders and casts himself upon God and claims the promise, "Lord, I may have it; it is for me," what do you think of him? Hasn't he a right to say, "I shall have it"?

Yes, beloved, if you are willing, and if you are ready, God is willing and ready to close the bargain at once. Yes, you can have it now; without any outburst of feeling, without any flooding of the heart with light, you may have it. To some it comes in that way, but to many it does not. As a quiet transaction of the surrendered will, you can lift up your heart in faith and say, "O God, I do give myself as an empty vessel to be filled with the Holy Spirit. I give myself up once and for all, for eternity." If you will take your place before God, you can repeat those lyrics, "'Tis done, the great transaction's done."

Ministers of the Gospel, have you never felt the need of being filled with the Holy Spirit? Your heart, perhaps, tells you that you know nothing of that blessing. Workers for Christ, have you never felt a need, "I must be filled with the Holy Spirit"? Children of God, have you never felt a hope rise within you, "I may have this blessing of which I hear from others"? Will you not take the step and say, "I shall have it"?

Say it, not in your own strength, but in self-despair. Never mind that it appears as if your heart is all cold and closed up; never mind that. But as an act of obedience and of surrender, as an act of the will, cast yourself before Jesus and trust Him. Say, "I shall have it, for I now give up myself into the arms of my Lord Jesus. I shall have it, for it is the delight of Jesus to give the Holy Spirit from the Father into the hearts of everyone. I shall have it, for I do believe in Jesus, and He promised me that out of him who believes shall *flow rivers of living water*' (John 7:38). I shall have it! I shall have it! I will cling to the feet of Jesus; I will stay at the throne of God; I shall have it, *for he is faithful that promised*' (Heb. 10:23)."

9

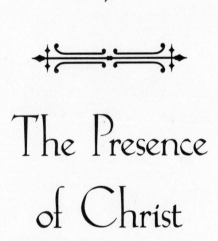

The Presence
of Christ

9

The Presence of Christ

*But straightway Jesus spake unto them,
saying, Be of good cheer; it is I;
be not afraid.*
—Matthew 14:27

It is from Christ Jesus that the Spirit comes to us; it is to Christ Jesus that the Spirit ever brings us; and the one need of the Christian life day by day and hour by hour is this: the presence of the Son of God. God is our salvation. If I have Christ with me and Christ in me, I have full salvation.

You have most likely heard much about the life of failure and of the flesh, about the life of unbelief and disobedience, about the life of ups and downs, the wilderness life of sadness and of sorrow; but I have heard, and I have believed, that there is deliverance. Bless God, He brought us out of Egypt so that He might bring us into Canaan, into the very rest of God and Jesus Christ.

"He is our peace" (Eph. 2:14); He is our rest. Oh, if I may only have the presence of Jesus as the victory over every sin, the presence of Jesus as the strength for every duty, then my life will be in the full sunshine of God's unbroken fellowship, and the word will be fulfilled to me in most blessed experience: *"Son, thou art ever with me, and all that I have is thine"* (Luke 15:31). My heart will answer, "Father, I never knew it, but it is true: I am always with You, and all that You have is mine."

God has given all He has to Christ, and He desires that Christ should have you and me entirely. I come to every hungry heart and say, "If you want to live to the glory of God, seek one thing: to claim, to believe, that the presence of Jesus can be with you every moment of your life."

I want to focus upon the presence of Jesus as it is set before us in that blessed story of

Christ's walking on the sea. Come and look with me at some lessons that are suggested to us.

The Presence Lost

Think, first, of the presence of Christ that was lost. You know the disciples loved Christ, clung to Him, and with all their failings delighted in Him. But what happened? The Master went up the mountain to pray, and He sent them across the sea all alone without Him. A storm came, and they toiled and rowed and labored, but the wind was against them. They made no progress; they were in danger of perishing. Their hearts cried, "If only the Master were here!" But His presence was gone. They missed Him. Once before, they had been in a storm, and Christ had said, *"Peace, be still"* (Mark 4:39), and all was well. But here they were in darkness, danger, and terrible trouble and had no Christ to help them.

Isn't that the life of many believers at times? We get into darkness, we have committed sin, the cloud is upon us, and we miss the face of Jesus. For days and days, we work, worry, and labor, but it is all in vain, for we miss the presence of Christ. Oh, beloved, write it down and do not forget it: the presence of Jesus lost is the cause of all our wretchedness and failure.

The Presence Feared

Look at the second step: the presence of Jesus feared. The disciples were longing for the presence of Christ, and Christ came after midnight. He came walking on the water amid the waves. But they did not recognize Him, and they cried out for fear, *"It is a spirit"* (Matt. 14:26). Their beloved Lord was coming near, and they did not know Him. They dreaded His approach. Oh, how often I have seen a believer dreading the approach of Christ, crying out for Him, longing for Him, and yet dreading His coming! And why? Because Christ came in a way that they had not expected.

Perhaps some have been saying, "Oh, I fear I can never have the abiding presence of Christ." You have heard people talk about a life in the Spirit; you have heard them talk about always abiding in the presence of God and in His fellowship, and you have been afraid of it. You have said, "It is too high and too difficult for me to reach." You have dreaded the very teaching that was going to help you. Jesus came to you in the teaching, and you did not recognize His love.

Or perhaps He came in a way that made you fear His presence. Perhaps God has been speaking to you about some sin. There is that sin of anger, that sin of unlovingness, that sin of unforgiveness, or that sin of worldliness, compromise, and fellowship with the world; that love of man and man's honor, that fear of man and man's opinion; that pride and self-confidence. God has been speaking to you about it, and you have been frightened. That was Jesus wanting to draw near, but you were afraid. You do not see how you can give up all that; you are not ready to say, "At any cost, I am going to have that taken out of me, and I will give it up." And while Christ was coming near to bless you, you were afraid of Him.

Oh, believers, at other times Christ has come to you with affliction, and perhaps you have said, "If I want to be entirely holy, I know I will have to be afflicted, but I am afraid of affliction." You have dreaded the thought that Christ may come to you in affliction. This is the presence of Christ feared.

Beloved, I want to tell you it is all misconception. The disciples had no reason to fear that *"spirit"* (Matt. 14:26), for it was Christ

Himself. When God's Word comes close to you and touches your heart, remember that is Christ out of whose mouth comes the two-edged sword. (See Revelation 1:16.) It is Christ in His love coming to cut away the sin, so that He may fill your heart with the blessing of God's love. Beware of fearing the presence of Christ.

The Presence Revealed

Then comes the third thought: the presence of Christ revealed. Bless God! When Christ heard how the disciples cried out, He spoke the words, *"Be of good cheer; it is I; be not afraid."* Ah, what gladness those words brought to those hearts! There is Jesus! There is that dark object, that dreaded form, and it is our blessed Lord Himself.

Dear friends, the Master's objective, whether it is by affliction or otherwise, is to prepare you for receiving the presence of Christ. Through it all, He says, *"It is I; be not afraid."* Oh, the presence of Christ revealed! I want to tell you, believer, that the Son of God is longing to reveal Himself to you. Listen! Listen! Do any of you have longing hearts? Jesus says, *"Be of good cheer; it is I; be not afraid."*

Beloved, God has given us Christ. Does God want us to have Christ every moment? Without a doubt. God wants the presence of Christ to be the joy of every hour of our lives; and if there is one thing that is sure, it is that Christ can reveal Himself to us every moment. Are you willing to come and claim this privilege?

Christ can reveal Himself. I cannot reveal Him to you; you cannot grasp Him; but He can shine into your heart. How can you know Christ? Christ can reveal Himself. And, before I go further, I pray that you will set your heart upon this and will offer the humble prayer, "Lord, now reveal Yourself to me, so that I may never lose the sight of You. Allow me to understand that, through the thick darkness, You come to make Yourself known."

Do not let your heart begin to doubt—however dark it may be, whatever midnight there may be in the soul—that Christ can reveal Himself at midnight, in the dark. Ah, thank God, often after ten or twenty years of struggling, sometimes in the light and sometimes in the dark, there comes a time when Jesus is willing to give Himself to us, never to part with us again. May God grant us that presence of Jesus!

The Presence Desired

And now comes the fourth thought. The presence of Jesus lost was the first; the presence of Jesus feared was the second; the presence of Jesus revealed was the third; the presence of Jesus desired is the fourth.

What happened? Peter heard the Lord, and he was content. Peter was in the boat, and there was Jesus, some thirty or forty yards away; He acted as if He would have passed them. Though Peter had terrible failure and carnality in him, he had his heart right with Christ, and he wanted to claim His presence. He said to Jesus, *"Lord, if it be thou, bid me come unto thee on the water"* (Matt. 14:28).

Yes, Peter could not rest; he wanted to be as near to Christ as possible. He saw Christ walking on the water; he remembered that Christ had said, *"Follow me"* (Matt. 4:19); he remembered how Christ, with the miraculous supply of fishes, had proved that He was Master of the sea and of the waters; and he remembered how Christ had stilled the storm. Without argument or reflection, all at once he said, "There is my Lord manifesting Himself in a new way. There is my Lord exercising a new and supernatural power, and I can go to my Lord. He is able to make me walk where He walks."

Peter wanted to walk as Christ did; he wanted to walk near Christ. He did not say, "Lord, let me walk around the sea here," but he said, "Lord, command me to come to You" (Matt. 14:28).

Friends, would you not like to have the presence of Christ in this way? Not that Christ would come down—that is what many Christians want. They want to continue in their sinful walks; they want to continue in their worldly walks; they want to continue in their old lives; at the same time, they want Christ to come down to them with His comfort, His presence, and His love. But that cannot be. If we are to have the presence of Christ, we must walk as He walked.

Christ's walk was a supernatural one. He walked in the love and power of God. Most people walk according to the circumstances in which they are living, and most people say, "I am depending upon circumstances for my religion." You hear people say a hundred times over, "My circumstances prevent me from enjoying unbroken fellowship with Jesus."

What were the circumstances that were around Christ? The wind and the waves— and Christ walked triumphantly over circumstances. Peter said, "Like my Lord, I can triumph over all circumstances. Anything around me is nothing, if I have Jesus." He longed for the presence of Christ. I pray to God that, as we look at the life of Christ upon earth, as we look at how Christ walked and conquered the waves, every one of us will be able to say, "I want to walk like Jesus." If that is your heart's desire, you can expect the presence of Jesus; but as long as you want to walk on a lower level than Christ, as long as you want to have a little of the world and a little of self-will, do not expect to have the presence of Christ.

Near Christ and like Christ—the two things go together. Have you taken that lesson into your heart? Peter wanted to walk like Christ so that he might get near Christ, and it is this I want to offer every one of you. I want to say even to the weakest believer, "With God's presence, you can have the presence and fellowship of Christ all day long, your whole life through." I want to bring you that promise, but I must give God's condition: walk like Christ, and you will always abide near Christ. The presence of Christ invites you to come and have unbroken fellowship with Him.

The Presence Trusted

Then comes the next thought. We have just discussed the presence of Christ desired, and my next thought is the presence of Christ trusted. When Peter asked Christ to command him to come to Him, the Lord Jesus said, *"Come"* (Matt. 14:29). And what did Peter do? He stepped out of the boat. How did he dare to do it against all the laws of nature? He sought Christ, he heard Christ's voice, he trusted Christ's presence and power, and in the faith of Christ he said, "I can walk on the water." So he stepped out of the boat.

Here is the turning point; here is the crisis. Peter saw Christ in the manifestation of a supernatural power, and Peter believed that that supernatural power could work in him and cause him to live a supernatural life. He believed this applied even to walking on the sea.

Here lies the whole secret of the life of faith: Christ has supernatural power—the power of heaven, the power of holiness, the power of fellowship with God—and Christ can give me grace to live as He lived. If I will, like Peter, simply look at Christ and say to Christ, "Lord, speak the word, and I will come," and if I will listen to Christ saying, "Come," I, too, will have power to walk upon the waves.

Have you ever seen a more beautiful and more instructive symbol of the Christian life? I once preached on it many years ago, and the thought that filled my heart then was this: the Christian life can be compared to Peter walking on the waves. There is nothing as difficult and impossible without Christ, nothing as blessed and safe with Christ. That is the Christian life: impossible without Christ's nearness, but most safe and blessed, however difficult it may be, if we have the presence of Christ.

Believers, I have tried in these words to call you to a better life, to a spiritual life, to a holy life, to a life in the Spirit, to a life in fellowship with God. There is only one thing that can enable you to live it: you must have the Lord Jesus holding your hand every minute of the day. "But is that possible?" you ask. Yes, it is. "I have so much to think about," you say. "Sometimes for four or five hours of the day I have to go into the very thick of business and have ten or more people standing around me, each claiming my attention. How can I, how can I *always,* have the presence of Jesus?" Beloved, this can happen because Jesus is your God, because He loves you wonderfully and is able to make His presence clearer to you than that of ten men who are standing around you.

If you will take time each morning and enter into your covenant with Him, saying, "My Lord Jesus, nothing can satisfy me but Your abiding presence," He will give it to you. He will surely give it to you. Peter trusted the presence of Christ, and he said, "If Christ calls me, I can walk on the waves to Him." Will you trust the presence of Christ?

To walk through all the circumstances and temptations of life is exactly like walking on the water: you have no solid ground under your feet, but you have the Word of God to rest on. You do not know how strong the temptations of Satan may be, but do believe that God wants you to walk in a supernatural life above human power. God wants you to live a life in Christ Jesus. Do you want to live that life? Come then, and say, "Jesus, I have heard Your promise that Your presence will go with me. You have said, *'My presence shall go with thee'* (Exod. 33:14). Lord, I claim it; I trust You."

The Presence Forgotten

Now, the sixth step in this wonderful series is the presence of Christ forgotten. Peter got out of the boat and began to walk toward the Lord Jesus with his eyes fixed upon Him. The presence of Christ was trusted by him, and he walked boldly over the waves; but all at once he took his eyes off Jesus, and he immediately began to sink. There was Peter, his walk of faith at an end, all drenched and drowning and crying out, *"Lord, save me"* (Matt. 14:30).

I know that some of you are saying in your hearts, "Ah, that is what will become of you higher-life Christians." There are people who say, "You can never live that life; do not talk of it; you must always be failing."

Peter always failed before the Day of Pentecost. It was because the Holy Spirit had not yet come. Peter's experience teaches us that while he was still in the life of the flesh, he had to fail somehow or other. But, thank God, there was One to lift him out of the failure. Out of that failure, he came into closer union with and deeper dependence upon Jesus than ever before. But let me say a little more about his failure.

Someone may say, "I have been trying to say, 'Lord, I will live it.' But suppose failure comes; what then?" Learn from Peter what you ought to do. What did Peter do? The very opposite of what most people do. What did he do when he began to sink? That very moment, without one word of self-reproach or self-condemnation, he cried out, *"Lord, save me"* (Matt. 14:30). I wish I could teach every Christian that.

I remember the time in my spiritual life when that became clear to me. Up to that time, when I failed, my only thought was to reproach and condemn myself, and I thought that would do me good. I found it did not do me good, and I learned from Peter that my duty is, the very moment I fail, to say, "Jesus, Master, help me!" And the very moment I say that, Jesus does help me.

Remember, failure is not an impossible situation. I can think of more than one Christian who said, "Lord, I claim the fullness of the Holy Spirit. I want to live every hour of every day filled with the Holy Spirit." And I can imagine an honest soul who said that with a trembling faith, yet he may have fallen. I want to say to that soul, "Don't be discouraged. If failure comes, immediately appeal to Jesus, without any waiting. He is always ready to hear."

The very moment you find there is a temper, a hasty word, or some other wrong, the living Jesus will immediately come near; He is so gracious and so mighty. Appeal to Him, and there will be help at once. If you will learn to do this, Jesus will lift you up and lead you on to a walk where His strength will secure you from failure.

The Presence Restored

And here is my last thought. The presence of Jesus had been forgotten while Peter looked at the waves; but now, lastly, we have the presence of Jesus restored. Yes, Christ stretched out His hand to save him. Possibly—for Peter was a very proud, self-confident man—possibly he had to sink so that he would learn that it was not his faith that could save him, but it was the power of Christ. God wants us to learn the lesson that when we fall, then we can cry to Jesus, and immediately He will reach out His hand. Remember, Peter walked back to the boat without sinking again. Why? Because Christ was very near to him.

Remember, it is quite possible, if you use your failure correctly, to be far nearer to Christ after it than before. Use it correctly, I say. That is, come and acknowledge, "In me there is nothing, but I am going to trust my Lord unboundedly." Let every failure teach you to cling afresh to Christ, and He will prove Himself a mighty and loving Helper.

The presence of Jesus restored! Yes, Christ took Peter by the hand and helped him, and I do not know whether they walked hand in hand those forty or fifty yards back to the boat or whether Christ allowed Peter to walk beside Him. But this I know: they were very near to each other, and it was the nearness to his Lord that strengthened Peter.

Remember what has taken place since that happened with Peter. The cross has been erected, the blood has been shed, the grave has been opened, the Resurrection has been accomplished, heaven has been opened, and the Spirit of the Exalted One has come down. Believe that it is possible for the presence of Jesus to be with us every day and all the time. Your God has given you Christ, and He wants to put Christ into your heart in such a way that His presence will be with you every moment of your life.

Who is willing to lift up his eyes and his heart and to exclaim, "I want to live according to God's standard"? Who is willing? Who is willing to cast himself into the arms of Jesus and to live a life of faith victorious over the winds and the waves, over the circumstances and difficulties? Who is willing to say, *"Lord...bid me come unto thee on the water"* (Matt. 14:28)? Are you willing? Listen! Jesus says, *"Come"* (v. 29). Will you step out at this moment?

The boat, the old life that Peter had been leading, was at a distance. He had been familiar with the sea from his boyhood, and that boat was a very sacred place. Christ had sat beside him there; Christ had preached from that boat. From that boat of Peter's, Christ had given the wonderful supply of fishes; it was a very sacred boat. But Peter left it to come to a place more sacred still, which consisted of walking with Jesus on the water—a new and a divine experience.

Your Christian life may be a very sacred thing. You may say, "Christ saved me by His blood; He has given me many experiences of grace. God has proven His grace in my heart." But you confess, "I don't have the real life of abiding fellowship; the winds and the waves often terrify me, and I sink." Oh, come out of the boat of past experiences at once; come out of the boat of external circumstances. Come out of the boat, step out on the word of Christ, and believe, "With Jesus I can walk upon the water."

When Peter was in the boat, what was between him and the bottom of the sea? Only a couple of planks. But when he stepped out upon the water, what was between him and the sea? Not a plank, but the word of the almighty Jesus. Will you come, and, without any experience, will you rest upon the word of Jesus: *"Lo, I am with you alway"* (Matt. 28:20)? Will you rest upon His word: *"Be of good cheer; it is I; be not afraid"*?

Jesus lives in heaven every moment. Jesus whispers that word every moment by His Spirit, and He lives every moment to make it true. Accept it now! My Lord Jesus is equal to every emergency. My Lord Jesus can meet the needs of every soul. My whole heart says, "He can, He can do it. He will, He will do it!" Oh, come, believers, and let us most deliberately, most quietly, most restfully claim it as our portion.

10

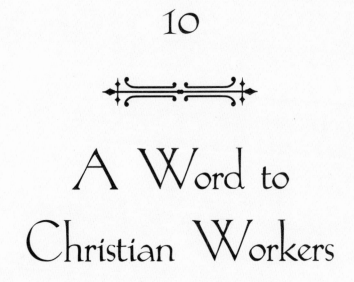

A Word to
Christian Workers

10

A Word to Christian Workers

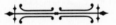

Some time ago, I read these words of William Law concerning ministers of the Gospel, but they apply to all Christians:

> After truly giving his heart over to God, who is the sole Creator of it, one must humbly beg that everything he hopes will be done in others under his influence, may first be truly and fully done in himself.

These words have stuck with me ever since. What a solemn application this is to the subject that occupied our attention in previous chapters: living and working under the fullness of the Holy Spirit! And yet, if we understand our calling correctly, every one of us will have to say, "That is the one thing on which everything depends."

What good is it to tell others that they may be filled with the Spirit of God, if, when they ask us, "Has God done it for you?" we have to answer, "No, He has not done it"? What good is it for me to tell others that Jesus Christ can dwell within us every moment and keep us from sin and actual transgression, and that the abiding presence of God can be our portion all day long, if I do not wait upon God first to do it truly and fully in myself each day?

Look at the Lord Jesus Christ. It was of the Christ Himself, when He had received the Holy Spirit from heaven, that John the Baptist said, *"He shall baptize you with the Holy Ghost"* (Matt. 3:11). I can only communicate to others what God has imparted to me. If my life as a minister is a life in which the flesh still greatly prevails, if my life is a life in which I grieve the Spirit of God, I can expect that my congregation will receive through me a very impure kind of life. But if the life of God dwells in me and I am filled with His power, then I can hope that the life that goes out from me may be infused into my hearers, too.

Why the Spirit Is Needed

I have referred to the need of every believer to be filled with the Spirit. What can be of deeper interest to us ministers and Christian workers now, or what can better occupy our attention, than to prayerfully consider how we can bring others to believe that this is possible, how we can lead every believer to seek it for himself, to expect it, and to accept it to the degree that he lives it out? But, fellow Christians, the message must come from us as a witness of our personal experience, by the grace of God. William Law said elsewhere,

> The first business of a minister, when he sees men awakened and brought to Christ, is to lead them to know the Holy Spirit.

How true! Do we not find this throughout the Word of God? John the Baptist preached Christ as the *"Lamb of God, which taketh away the sin of the world"* (John 1:29). We read in Matthew that he also said that Christ would *"baptize...with the Holy Ghost, and with fire"* (Matt. 3:11). In the gospel of John, we read that John the Baptist was told that he would see the Spirit descending and abiding upon Him who would baptize with the Spirit. Thus John the Baptist led the people on from Christ to the expectation of receiving the Holy Spirit for themselves.

And what did Jesus do? For three years, He was with His disciples, teaching and instructing them. But when He was about to go away, in His farewell discourse on the last night, what was His great promise to the disciples? *"I will pray the Father, and he shall give you another Comforter...the Spirit of truth"* (John 14:16–17). He had previously promised to those who believed on Him that *"rivers of living water"* (John 7:38) would flow from them, which the Evangelist explained as meaning the Holy Spirit: *"This spake he of the Spirit"* (v. 39). But this promise was only to be fulfilled after Christ was glorified.

Christ pointed to the Holy Spirit as the one fruit of being glorified. The glorified Christ leads to the Holy Spirit. So, in the Farewell Discourse, Christ led the disciples to expect the Spirit as the Father's great blessing. Then again, when Christ came and stood at the footstool of His heavenly throne, on the Mount of Olives, ready to ascend, what were His words? *"Ye shall receive power, after that the Holy Ghost is come upon you: and ye shall be witnesses unto me"* (Acts 1:8).

Christ's constant work was to teach His disciples to expect the Holy Spirit. Look through the book of Acts, and you will see the same thing. Peter, on the Day of Pentecost, preached that Christ was exalted and had received from the Father the promise of the Holy Spirit. And so he told the people,

> *Repent, and be baptized every one of you in the name of Jesus Christ for the remission of sins, and ye shall receive the gift of the Holy Ghost.* (Acts 2:38)

When I believe in Jesus risen, ascended, and glorified, I will receive the Holy Spirit.

Look again: after Philip had preached the Gospel in Samaria, men and women had been converted, and there was great joy in the city. The Holy Spirit had been working, but something was still lacking. Peter and John came down from Jerusalem, prayed for the converted ones, and laid their hands upon them. Then *"they received the Holy Ghost"* (Acts 8:17). They had the conscious possession and enjoyment of the Spirit; but until that came, they were incomplete. Paul was converted by the mighty power of Jesus, who appeared to him on the way to Damascus; yet he had to go to Ananias before he received the Holy Spirit.

We read that as Peter preached to Cornelius, *"the Holy Ghost fell on all them which heard the word"* (Acts 10:44). Peter took this as the sign that these Gentiles were one with the Jews in the favor of God, having the same baptism.

And so, we might go through many of the Epistles and still find the same truth taught. Look at that wonderful epistle to the Romans. The doctrine of justification by faith is established in the first five chapters. Then in the sixth and seventh chapters, we read that though the believer is represented as dead to sin and the law, and as married to Christ, a dreadful struggle goes on in the heart of the regenerate man as long as he has not gotten the full power of the Holy Spirit.

But in the eighth chapter, we find that it is the *"law of the Spirit of life in Christ Jesus"* (Rom. 8:2) that makes us free from *"the law of sin and death"* (v. 2). Then we are *"not in the flesh, but in the Spirit"* (v. 9), with the Spirit of God dwelling in us. All the teaching leads up to the Holy Spirit.

Again, look at the epistle to the Galatians. We always speak of the doctrine of justification by faith as the central truth of this epistle, but have you ever noticed how the doctrine of the Holy Spirit holds a most prominent place there? Paul asked the Galatian church, *"Received ye the Spirit by the works of the law, or by the hearing of faith?"* (Gal. 3:2). It was the *"hearing of faith"* that led them to the full enjoyment of the Spirit's power. *"We through the Spirit wait for the hope of righteousness by faith"* (Gal. 5:5). And then at the end of the fifth chapter, we are told, *"If we live in the Spirit, let us also walk in the Spirit"* (v. 25).

If we go to the epistles to the Corinthians, we find that Paul asked the Christians in Corinth, *"Know ye not that your body is the temple of the Holy Ghost which is in you?"* (1 Cor. 6:19).

If we look into the epistle to the Ephesians, we find the doctrine of the Holy Spirit mentioned twelve times. It is the Spirit who seals God's people: *"Ye were sealed with that holy Spirit of promise"* (Eph. 1:13). Through Christ, both Jew and Gentile *"have access by one Spirit unto the Father"* (Eph. 2:18). They are *"builded together for an habitation of God through the Spirit"* (v. 22). They are *"strengthened with might by his Spirit in the inner man"* (Eph. 3:16). *"With all lowliness and meekness, with longsuffering, forbearing one another in love;* [they endeavor] *to keep the unity of the Spirit in the bond of peace* (Eph. 4:2–3).

By not grieving *"the holy Spirit of God"* (Eph. 4:30), we preserve our sealing to *"the day of redemption"* (v. 30). Being *"filled with the Spirit"* (Eph. 5:18), we sing and make melody in our hearts to the Lord (v. 19) and thus glorify Him. Just study these epistles carefully, and you will find that what I say is true: the apostle Paul took great pains to lead Christians to the enjoyment of the Holy Spirit as the consummation of the Christian life.

It was the Holy Spirit who was given to the church at Pentecost, and it is the Holy Spirit who gives Pentecostal blessings now. It was this power, given to bless men, that brought about such wonderful life, love, and self-sacrifice in the early church. It is this that makes us look back to those days as the most beautiful part of the church's history. And it is the same Spirit of power that must dwell in the hearts of all believers in our day to bring the church to its true position.

Let us ask God, then, that every Christian minister and worker may be filled with the power of the Holy Spirit, that He may search us and try us and enable us to sincerely answer the question, "Have I known the indwelling and the filling of the Holy Spirit that God wants me to have?"

Let each one of us ask himself, "Is it my one goal to know the Holy Spirit dwelling in me, so that I may help others to yield to the same indwelling of the Holy Spirit, so that He may reveal Christ fully in them in His divine saving and keeping power?" Will not everyone have to confess, "Lord, I have all too little understood this; I have all too little manifested this in my work and preaching"?

Beloved, remember the principles set forth in the words of William Law:

> After truly giving his heart over to God, who is the sole Creator of it, one must humbly beg that everything he hopes will be done in others under his influence, may first be truly and fully done in himself.

And his first duty toward those who are awakened and brought to Christ is to lead them on to the full knowledge of the presence and indwelling of the Holy Spirit.

Three Questions

Who Will Acknowledge the Spirit?

If we are indeed to come into full harmony with these two great principles, we must answer some very important questions. The first question is, Why does the church of Christ have so little practical acknowledgment of the power of the Holy Spirit? I am not writing to you, my readers, as if I thought you were not sound in doctrine on this point. I write to you as to those who believe in the Holy Spirit as the third person in the ever blessed Trinity. But I write to you confidently, as to those who will also readily admit that the truth of the presence and of the power of the Holy Spirit is not acknowledged in the church as it ought to be.

Then the question is, Why is it not so acknowledged? I answer, because of its spiritual nature. It is one of the most difficult truths in the Bible for the human mind to comprehend. God has revealed Himself in creation throughout the whole universe. He has revealed Himself in Christ incarnate—and what a subject of study the person, word, and works of Christ form! But how much more difficult it is to comprehend the mysterious indwelling of the Holy Spirit, hidden in the depths of the life of the believer!

In the early Pentecostal days of the church, this knowledge was intuitive; believers possessed the Spirit in power. But soon afterward, the *"spirit of the world"* (1 Cor. 2:12) began to creep into the church and mastered it. This was followed by the deeper darkness of formality and superstition, when the spirit of the world completely triumphed in what was improperly called the church of Christ.

The Reformation in the days of Luther restored the truth of justification by faith in Christ, but the doctrine of the Holy Spirit did not then obtain its proper place, for God does not reveal all truth at one time. A great deal of the spirit of the world was still left in the reformed churches. But now God is awakening the church to strive after a fuller and more scriptural understanding of the Holy Spirit's place and power. Through the means of books, discussions, and conventions, many hearts are being stirred.

Brothers and sisters, it is our privilege to take part in this great movement; let us therefore engage in the work more earnestly than ever. Let each of us say, "My great work is in preaching Christ, to lead men to acknowledge the Holy Spirit, who alone can glorify Christ." I may try to glorify Christ in my preaching, but it will avail nothing without the Spirit of God. I may urge men to the practice of holiness and every Christian virtue, but all my persuasion will avail very little unless

I help them to believe that they have the Holy Spirit dwelling in them every moment, enabling them to live the life of Christ.

The great reason why the Holy Spirit was given from heaven was to make Christ Jesus' presence manifest to us. While Jesus was incarnate, His disciples were too much under the power of the flesh to allow Christ to take up residence in their hearts. It was necessary, said Christ, that He go away, so that the Spirit might come. (See John 16:7.) Jesus promised that He would come with the Spirit, and the Father would also come, and they would make their abode in the hearts of those who loved Him and kept His commandments. (See John 14:23.)

It is therefore the Holy Spirit's great work to reveal the Father and the Son in the hearts of God's people. If we believe and teach men that the Holy Spirit can make Christ a reality to them every moment, men will learn to believe and accept Christ's presence and power, of which they now know far too little.

What Can We Expect?

Then another question presents itself, namely, What are we to expect when the Holy Spirit is duly acknowledged and received? I ask this question because there is something I have frequently noticed with considerable interest—and, I may say, with some anxiety. I sometimes hear men praying earnestly for a baptism of the Holy Spirit, so that He may give them power for their Christian work. Beloved brothers and sisters, we need this power, not only for work, but also for our daily lives. Remember, we must have it all the time.

In Old Testament times, the Spirit came with power upon the prophets and other inspired men, but He did not dwell permanently in them. In the same way, in the church of the Corinthians, the Holy Spirit came with power to work miraculous gifts, yet they had only a small measure of His sanctifying grace. You will remember the carnal strife, envying, and divisions that were there. They had gifts of utterance, gifts of knowledge and wisdom, and so on, but pride, unlovingness, and other sins sadly marred the character of many of them. And what does this teach us? That a man may have a great gift of power for Christian work, but very little of the indwelling Spirit.

In 1 Corinthians, we are reminded that although we may have faith that can move mountains, if we do not have love, we are nothing (1 Cor. 13:2). We must have the love that brings the humility and self-sacrifice of Jesus. We should not put too much emphasis on the gifts we may possess; if we do, we will have very little blessing. But we should seek, in the first place, that the Spirit of God will come as a light and power of holiness through the presence of the indwelling Jesus. Let the first work of the Holy Spirit be to humble you deep down in the very dust, so that your whole life will be a tender, brokenhearted waiting on God, in the consciousness of mercy coming from above.

Do not seek large gifts; there is something deeper that you need. It is not enough that a tree shoots its branches to the sky and is covered thickly with leaves; we want its roots to strike deeply into the soil. Let the thought of the Holy Spirit's being in us, and our hope of being filled with the Spirit, be always accompanied in us by broken and contrite hearts. Let us bow very low before God, waiting for His grace to fill and sanctify us.

While our inner man remains unsanctified, we do not need a power that God might allow us to use. We need God to give us full possession of Himself. In due time, the special gift may come, but we need first and now the power of the Holy Spirit, working something far mightier and more effective in us than any such gift. We should seek, therefore, not only a baptism of power, but also a baptism of holiness. We should seek that the inner nature be sanctified by the indwelling of Jesus, and then other power will come as needed.

Remain Steadfast

There is a third question. Suppose someone says to me, "I have given myself up to be filled with the Spirit, and I do not feel that there is any difference in my condition. There is no change of experience that I can speak of. What must I then think? Mustn't I think that my surrender was not honest?" No, do not think that. "But what, then? Does God give no response?" Beloved, God gives a response, but it is not always within certain months or years. "What, then, would you have me to do?" I will answer you, "You must retain the position you have taken before God and maintain it every day." Say, "Oh, God, I have given myself to be filled. Here I am, an empty vessel, trusting and expecting to be filled by You."

Take that position every day and every hour. Ask God to write it across your heart.

Give up to God an empty, consecrated vessel, so that He may fill it with the Holy Spirit. Take that position constantly. It may be that you are not fully prepared. Ask God to cleanse you, to give you grace to separate you from everything sinful—from unbelief or whatever hindrance there may be. Then take your position before God and say, "My God, You are faithful. I have entered into a covenant with You for Your Holy Spirit to fill me, and I believe You will fulfill it."

Brothers and sisters, I say for myself, for every minister of the Gospel, and for every fellow worker, man or woman, that if we thus come before God with a full surrender, in a bold, believing attitude, God's promise must be fulfilled.

If you were to ask me about my own experience, I would say this: there have been times when I hardly knew what to think of God's answer to my prayer in this matter. But I have found it my joy and my strength to maintain my position and say, "My God, I have given myself up to You. It was Your own grace that led me to Christ, and I stand before You in confidence that You will keep Your covenant with me to the end. I am the empty vessel; You are the God who fills all." God is faithful, and He gives the promised blessing in His own time and method. Beloved, for His sake, be content with nothing less than full health and a full spiritual life. *"Be filled with the Spirit"* (Eph. 5:18).

Let me return now to the two expressions with which I began. The first was,

> After truly giving his heart over to God, who is the sole Creator of it, one must humbly beg that everything he hopes will be done in others under his influence, may first be truly and fully done in himself.

Friends, I ask you, is it not the longing of your hearts to have a congregation of believers filled with the Holy Spirit, to see others filled with His presence? Is it not your unceasing prayer for the church of Christ in which you minister that the Spirit of holiness, the very Spirit of God's Son, the Spirit of unworldliness and of heavenly-mindedness, may possess it? Is it not your desire that the Spirit of victory and of power over sin may fill its children? If you are willing for that to come, your first duty is to have it yourself.

And then the second expression stated that the first duty of every Christian worker is to lead those who have been brought to Christ to be entirely filled with the Holy Spirit. How can I do my work with success? I can imagine what a privilege it is to be led by the Spirit of God in all that I am doing. In studying my Bible, praying, visiting, organizing, or whatever I am doing, God is willing to guide me by His Holy Spirit. It sometimes becomes a humiliating experience to me that I am impatient and do not wait for the blessing. When that is the case, God can bring me back again.

But there is also the blessed experience of God guiding me with His hand, often through deep darkness, by His Holy Spirit. Let us walk among the people as men of God, so that we may not only tell others about a book we have read and what we believe with our hearts to be true, but we may also show what we are and what we have in our own experience.

Jesus called us witnesses for Him (Acts 1:8). What does that mean? The Holy Spirit brought down from heaven and gave to men a participation in the glory and the joy of the exalted Christ. Peter and the others who spoke with Jesus were filled with this heavenly Spirit, and thus Christ spoke in them and accomplished the work for them.

Oh, dear readers, if you and I are Christ's, we should take our places and claim our privileges. We are witnesses to the truth that we believe, witnesses to the reality of what Jesus does and what He is, by His presence in our own souls. If we are willing to be such witnesses for Christ, let us go to our God; let us make confession and surrender and, by faith, claim what God has for us as ministers of the Gospel and workers in His service. God will prove faithful. Even at this very moment, He will touch our hearts with a deep consciousness of His faithfulness and of His presence, and He will give to every hungering, trustful one what he continually needs.

About the Author

Andrew Murray (1828–1917) was an amazingly prolific Christian writer. He lived and ministered as both a pastor and author in the towns and villages of South Africa. Some of Murray's earliest works were written to provide nurture and guidance to Christians, whether young or old in the faith; they were actually an extension of his pastoral work. Once books such as *Abide in Christ, Like Christ,* and *With Christ in the School of Prayer* were written, Murray became widely known, and new books from his pen were awaited with great eagerness throughout the world.

He wrote to give daily practical help to many of the people in his congregation who lived out in the farming communities and could only come into town for church services on rare occasions. As he wrote these books of instruction, Murray adopted the practice of placing many of his more devotional books into thirty-one separate readings to correspond with the days of the month.

At the age of seventy-eight, Murray resigned from the pastorate and devoted most of his time to his manuscripts. He continued to write profusely, moving from one book to the next with an intensity of purpose and a zeal that few men of God have ever equaled. He often said of himself, rather humorously, that he was like a hen about to hatch an egg; he was restless and unhappy until he got the burden of the message off his mind.

During these later years, after hearing of pocket-sized paperbacks, Andrew Murray immediately began to write books to be published in that fashion. He thought it was a splendid way to have the teachings of the Christian life at your fingertips, where they could be carried around and read at any time of the day.

One source has said of Andrew Murray that his prolific style possesses the strength and eloquence that are born of deep earnestness and a sense of the solemnity of the issues of the Christian life. Nearly every page reveals an intensity of purpose and appeal that stirs men to the depths of their souls. Murray moves the emotions, searches the conscience, and reveals the sins and shortcomings of many of us with a love and hope born out of an intimate knowledge of the mercy and faithfulness of God.

For Andrew Murray prayer was considered our personal home base from which we live our Christian lives and extend ourselves to others. During his later years, the vital necessity of unceasing prayer in the spiritual life came to the forefront of Andrew Murray's teachings. It was then that he revealed the secret treasures of his heart concerning a life of persistent and believing prayer.

Countless people the world over have hailed Andrew Murray as their spiritual father and given credit for much of their Christian growth to the influence of his priceless devotional books.